The Road to My Farm

The
Road to My
Farm

Nora Janssen Seton

VIKING

VIKING
Published by the Penguin Group
Penguin Books USA Inc., 375 Hudson Street,
New York, New York 10014, U.S.A.
Penguin Books Ltd, 27 Wrights Lane,
London W8 5TZ, England
Penguin Books Australia Ltd, Ringwood,
Victoria, Australia
Penguin Books Canada Ltd, 10 Alcorn Avenue,
Toronto, Ontario, Canada M4V 3B2
Penguin Books (N.Z.) Ltd, 182–190 Wairau Road,
Auckland 10, New Zealand

Penguin Books Ltd, Registered Offices:
Harmondsworth, Middlesex, England

First published in 1993 by Viking Penguin
a division of Penguin Books USA Inc.

1 3 5 7 9 10 8 6 4 2

The author has changed the names of certain individuals
described in this book.

Portions of this book first appeared, in different form,
in *Eating Reading* and *Greenwich News*.

LIBRARY OF CONGRESS CATALOGING IN PUBLICATION DATA
Seton, Nora Janssen.
The road to my farm / Nora Janssen Seton.
p.   cm.
ISBN 0-670-84514-0
1. Seton, Nora Janssen.   2. Farmers—New England—Biography.
3. Women farmers—New England—Biography.   I. Title.
S417.S44A3   1993
630'.92—dc20
[B]   92-50770

Printed in the United States of America
Set in Galliard
Designed by Kathryn Parise

*This book is dedicated to my
mother and father.*

Whatsoever thy hand findeth to do,
do it with thy might.

ECCLESIASTES 9:10

Acknowledgments

I am indebted to Texas A&M and the indefatigable Aggie spirit which embraced and nurtured me during my years in College Station. My special thanks to Ron Knutson, a true mentor, and to Carl and Peggy Shafer, who gave me the intangibles.

This book is a consequence of the counsel and encouragement of family, friends, farmers, merchants, and millers, to whom I'm very grateful.

Of course, there would be no such book were there not Kathryn, Caroline, and John.

Contents

The
Road to My
Farm

Prologue

The Own Farm Overture

"Oh, *don't* be a farmer," said a friend of mine. "Everybody's fed up with farmers nowadays. Farmers are poisoning the American food supply. And they won't give their grain to millions of starving refugees in the Sudan. I read that somewhere."

It was a perfect, crisp October day in 1988, and we had been spending the afternoon touring the autumn colors of the Vermont countryside. My friend had picked up several items along the way, toys for her young children, folk art for her living room, a gift for her mother-in-law. There were: a wooden cow on wheels with a pulling string; an old cast-iron cornbread mold with the shapes of corn cobs; a copper reproduction of an early American rooster weather vane; some note cards with colorful images of grazing barnyard animals.

Her thoughts had followed mine.

"Farms have changed," she said. "They used to be nice places full of different animals making nice squawks. Farmers were American heroes, Noble Savages, tillers of the land and all that. They raised healthy crops without all the chemicals and their cows were, you know, happy.

"But it's all over. Farming's become a different thing. Farmers are destroying the soil. They need the drug and chemical companies to keep the ground producing anything. They dope up their animals to make them grow unnaturally fast. They're polluting the national water supplies. And, I'll tell you what—they don't even let animals have sex anymore. It's all done with pipettes and tanks of frozen sperm.

"It's all different, believe me. It's not like it looks in the picture books, and it bears little relation to your agribusiness experience, I'll bet, if that's what you're thinking. I don't understand how you could just up and do this."

We had come from Woodstock and were driving southward, along fallowed fields of blond stubble and small, discrete meadows sprinkled gently with white sheep. In the autumn, New England farmland turns almost stoic. I love the monkish quiet after the exuberant blossoms of summer and before the mantling cold of winter.

"Well," I said, "we're not approaching this rashly. But we're pretty serious. I have to do some investigating first."

We passed a field dotted with grids of two-foot fir trees. This belonged to the Christmas tree business of the Northeast. Most of these saplings, after four or five years, would be spiral-bound and trucked to the sidewalks of East Coast cities. It is a lucrative business, I was thinking, particularly with older and more majestic trees, and even more so on the "cut-your-own" acres, where buyers deliriously pay extra to hack down and haul away their own trees. The cut-your-own/pick-your-own farms, I reflected, had emerged as a pretty savvy way to go.

"Vegetables might be nice," said my friend, nestling into the possibilities. "What you didn't feed to your animals, you could eat."

I sighed.

She sighed, too: "Everything looks so healthy up here. If you're going to farm, do it this way. Do it like they do in Vermont."

Vermont's got a good thing going. Anything it touches seems to turn natural shades of nice. In the 1980s rush to find healthful food products, retailers figured out straightaway that all a shelf item needed was the word *Vermont* on the label, and presto, off it went into the basket of certified organic sundries. Not just maple syrup. Not just cheddar cheese. Why constrain the Green Mountain entrepreneur? Out of the closet came Vermont coffees, Vermont salsas, Vermont champagne mustards. Sales of these products exceeded anyone's imagination—and imagination plays a sizable role in the interchange between buyers and sellers of food.

"I'll bet people up here don't use chemicals on their farms," mused my friend.

"Well, it's hard to generalize," I said. "I think a lot depends on what you're up against. Soil depletion. Livestock viruses. Crop pests."

She said, "No. I think up here, where it's not so industrialized—where it's families farming—people don't use chemicals because their kids could get hurt. Or their wells would be contaminated. Oh, look," she pointed. "There's a brown sheep over there. Brown sheep. Things are always so much more natural in Vermont."

·

My own background was not one of farming; it was barely rural. I was raised in Northampton, Massachusetts, a college town in the Berkshires, within a family whose sphere of intellectual inquiry extended into several arts and several sciences—but not those of agriculture, aesthetic as they were. My parents emphasized a classical education for all five of their children, and for me that led to Harvard University, where I stumbled through the odes of Propertius and mulled over the ancient coins of Greece. It might have been a tidy story, beginning with the liberal arts and metamorphosing eventually into some less liberal but pragmatic and remunerative career.

But my mother died as I was finishing up at Harvard, and then all the premises changed.

"I hope that this period of mourning," wrote one of my advisers, "will give way to a renewed sense of purpose." These words stand even today as one of the most important aids to my thinking. Purpose, I thought. The rebuilding of an internal scaffolding. Out of the ashes.

Several months after graduating from college, while dabbling without heart in a sequence of professional distractions, I got lucky. A swarm of hitherto unconnected aspirations suddenly collided (the Big Bang Theory of career development), and the outcome was not unlike the creation of a new private universe: agriculture, whatever that was. The idea seemed at first foreign to most of my family and friends, but they came to see that it made sense for me in terms of my interest in rural development, environmental resources, politics, and animals—cattle, primarily. When I announced that I had enrolled to study agricultural sciences at Texas A&M University, one of my sisters said, delighted, "Oh, cow college! What a great idea."

By coming relatively late to agriculture, my predisposition and academic credentials were different from those of most of my colleagues and professors. My ways of thinking about agrarian problems and achievements were considered at times heretical, at times innovative, at times useful, and at times altogether comical. My perspective matured, for obvious reasons, with more detachment than that of my peers, most of whom had grown up in the midst of agrarian communities.

As the daughter of a psychoanalyst, I suppose I would say that I developed a complex affection for American agriculture. I have admired its struggle to advance, to shed the constraining yokes of its history and the social romance that surrounds it. I once even aspired to become the secretary of agriculture, to help unknot and rebuild what I saw as a tangled and foundering entity. Even now I would hold a lingering ambition for that job, were I still as ignorant of the bureaucracy and unprogressive spirit embodied by the vast United States Department of Agriculture. But the USDA is a politically administered branch of our government and thus one whose deportment is not responsible to basic economic principles or consumer-oriented preferences; its policies are tolerated to remain in conflict while its programs grow increasingly expensive and corpulent. In my mind, agriculture is the fat and unhappy adolescent whose parents, wishing their child had turned out otherwise, pitch him more food to keep him, at least, hushed.

"You've put agriculture on the couch," said a friend.

.

Farming creeps into the American dream with surprising frequency. Most of us at one time or another have fantasized about it. Cashing in on the local mesclun market. A few chickens in the yard, like grandfather once had. Some glorious stallions tossing their silky manes around the meadow. Corn tassels as far as the eye can see. Two longhorns for effect in the front forty. And, apart from the pleasing visual images, farming has been viewed as an inherently healthy way of life, studded with moral lessons for children and good, solid work for adults. Despite modern soul-destroying realities along the lines of chemical herbicides and slaughterhouse (dis)assembly lines, this is the image that survives in the minds of America's nonfarm population, the ninety-eight percent of us 250 million whose only connection with the plough is through childhood stories and the charm of folk art renderings. We have coveted these impressions and hold ourselves above many of today's industrialized agricultural practices: "Not me. Oh, no. I wouldn't do it that way." Ultimately, however, most of us don't do it at all.

When I became involved with agriculture, I was startled by the degree of interest in it that lay simmering among friends, family, and acquaintances. It was as though I had flushed from the bush a hundred starling musings. There was a thirst for stories about the agrarian ethic, the bucolic aesthetic, the comedy of the barnyard and the miracle of calving. I probably bridled a bit; I don't remember. I have never had much patience with people getting sentimental about other lifestyles. For me, it distorts or denies the reality of those lifestyles—complex, unhappy, or splendid as they may be. What I loved about farming was the straightforward way it managed to combine the primordial chores of sowing and harvesting, and the warm-blooded conviction of animals like sheep, with the highly advanced machinery and technologies that have been steadily rattling the rest of society's bones. Agriculture makes a science of life and death, without removing a sense of either the miraculous or the melancholy.

Sometime during the years I spent in agribusiness, I became seriously interested in setting up a farm myself. My husband and I were planning to start a family, and apart from feeling pulled to farming, we thought it would be a felicitous, healthy context in which to raise children. I thought I could do it better—more efficiently, more humanely, more productively than others—and I believe a person needs to feel that way about any such embarkation. So I began to research the idea, at first with trepidation, then more forthrightly. I explored farming as plain food production, as a lifestyle, and as a source of personal meaning. I took in the myths and befriended a few unwelcome vulnerabilities. I looked at the broad picture and then I looked inside myself. This is how it looked.

Part One

Food Maker

1

The Seedstock of the Farmer

The desire to start a farm had plagued me for years. I say "plague" because for some time it really irked me—it didn't fit in properly with my image of myself, my background, or my professional goals. What was all that education for? How could I sacrifice my career? What did I know about the rudiments of ploughing a field or husbanding livestock? Was this some sort of fleeting romance? What if it failed?

And then I heard another voice: "Why are you always fighting with yourself?"

That was my father. Eventually, it also became the voice of my husband, a man who likewise didn't cotton to my internal battles, and who liked the idea of raising crops and livestock—particularly lamb—as much as I did. It was then that the fighting stopped, and the planning precipitated and the whole journey toward starting a farm began. For me, it has been both illuminating and exciting. The process has involved on the one hand a searching backward, to find the origin of my own penchant for farming, and on the other hand a searching forward, to project myself into the modern realities of small-scale agriculture.

The farm I had in mind comprised both crop and livestock

production. I imagined a small operation, old-fashioned in the sense of raising a little bit of everything. I wanted cattle and goats and poultry, my husband wanted sheep, and we both were interested in trying our hands at raising vegetables and maybe cultivating some fruit trees. That might sound extravagant if not far-fetched, given the current propensity toward monoculture and cash crops. In fact, it is altogether conceivable.

I looked upon the venture with a great excitement about the unknown: I hoped to learn from season to season, keep a farm journal that would itself mature into my yearly guide. I daydreamed about cultivating watercress, which my mother had loved, or curious salad greens for the area restaurateurs. I envisioned my farm on the rolling hilltops of northwest Connecticut, or maybe in Virginia. If it were Virginia, I wondered, would I feel compelled to grow okra? One had to be open-minded, I kept reminding myself, not yet knowing the particular constraints of soil or community.

"Open-minded?" my husband smiled, his eyes wide. "This is indeed a pivotal moment. But bok choy, bean sprouts, hot chilies, and rabbits for meat? How open-minded are you going to be?"

"Well," I said, "within practical boundaries. If we end up buying a farm with a sizable rock ledge, say, I might expand the goat idea. If we move to Texas, I might consider the cotton option. That's what I mean by open-minded. Adapting to the land as opposed to tailoring it. I don't want to buy swampland with the intention of filling it in and I don't want to buy mountainside with the intention of blasting it into a steppe."

"I feel the same way." He paused. "With one exception. The cotton. No cotton. I've heard plenty about cotton and I just don't think I could survive it."

I had indeed been reading up on cotton and making observations to my husband about the laborious process of raising it (it is temperamental), protecting it (it is prized by several bugs), weeding it (hoeing the rows is called "chopping" and is widely recognized as rugged, nightmarish work) and harvesting it (the recipe: one good crop dusting of chemicals for killing off the foliage; one enormous air-conditioned tractor for collecting the fluffy bolls from the dried-out plants; and one medical insurance policy with a low premium). But after a few days of discussing how taxing cotton production seemed, my husband and I finally agreed we might try it.

"Okay," he smiled. "Cotton. Even the image is slightly addictive." He added sarcastically, "I have a feeling I'm going to find out why our forefathers embraced slavery the way they did."

"I'll just plant a couple of rows," I said. "You can gin it in the kitchen. What a great idea."

This change of heart over cotton really characterized my husband's and my attitude about the farm. We were curious. Everything seemed worth a chance, worth investigation. Whatever crops we might intend to sell for income, we would grow others as well just to learn. I wanted to sense for myself the rhythms of cotton and kumquats, herbs and potatoes. Our field rows would be bordered with miscellany. And then, of course, there would be the animals. The keeping of livestock—most specifically, cattle and goats—alongside our crops best embodied my farm plan. I was drawn to the Jeffersonian ideals of diversity and complementarity. The notion of a motley barnyard with its spectrum of crops and livestock appealed to me. Each species has its own intrinsic rhythm, its own season, as we all do.

Although my husband and I agreed in principle about having a farm, we didn't just quit our jobs and head for Maine. We decided to keep working to save a little extra income for putting toward the future expense. There is an old joke in agricultural circles about a farmer who won a million-dollar lottery. Asked what he would do with all that money, the farmer said, "Oh, I guess I'll just keep on farming until it runs out." We accepted the humor of this story as well as the moral, and we decided to gather information over the next few years as we waited for an auspicious moment to buy our farm.

There was certainly time to think things through, since we were living at that point in the affluent community of Greenwich, Connecticut, just over the border from what demographers aptly dub the "major metropolitan area" of New York City—a sprawl of densely populated suburbs. In a town where property values stretched easily into the millions, we were comfortably ensconced in a small guest cottage on an ample estate. We loved the coziness of the cottage—coziness in the sense of tiny, since "cozy" in the sense of snugly insulated it was not. It was a terrific place for a couple actively extending their honeymoon into a third year. For people like this, carpenter ant infestations and breezes wafting through the walls are trifling matters.

One day, after settling a second fluffy layer of fiberglass insulation (upside-down, which shows how I deal with printed instructions) along the attic rafters, I sat out on the front stoop to have a cup of coffee and wash the glass dust down my throat. We had two petite garden plots on either side of the front door. They were meticulously laid out and wood-chipped, and I noticed a lone green plant poking up willfully among the clods of bark. Presuming that it didn't belong to The Plan of the estate's gardens, I permitted curiosity its rein and set myself to an investigation. I dug down around the stem for two inches before I bumped into a knob, a tuber of sorts. It was easily exhumed along with its knotty web of white roots and surprised worms.

"Who are you and where did you come from?" I murmured, prone to animism in my solitary hours. No answer—the inevitable pitfall of animism.

"Weed," I decided, stung by what I took as its tacit indictment of my sanity. But as I examined this plant, I suddenly saw in it an analogy to my decision about farming. Here was this robust yearning for a farm, I reflected, poking up in the midst of an otherwise nonagrarian life. If I burrowed down, maybe I would find the seed of this predilection, maybe I would be able to discern the roots of the idea itself. In the end, I would at least be better informed about what farming actually entailed, what kind of lifestyle and fulfillment it might provide.

And there was one other issue of which the plant incident made me mindful: I had and have now very mixed feelings about plants. Individually, or in small numbers, I don't much like them at all. Flower gardens especially tend to make me uneasy. I expect blooms to turn to pillars of salt if I look at them too long. The fragility and silence of all that foliage and petalry fills me with apprehensions. I have no inherent way with plants, and I speculate that it is only in spite of me that a few potted ivies have ever survived my ministry.

This pathology, however, is somehow divorced in my head from farm crops. At the same time that I will flinch from a breathtaking begonia, I can envision an acre of lettuce with confident pleasure and anticipation. Unearthing long furrows of fresh red potatoes transports me, gives me the thrill of an archaeologist. Beets are borderline, tomatoes I don't like staking, but most other vegetables I can readily conceive of cultivating on a scale of acres. In short, farming to my mind is completely and favorably removed from the negotiations of a house or garden plant. There is strength for me in the image of mass. I think that a field of sunflowers, soybeans, or pumpkins is a chorus of vigor.

As for whatever green life form I had yanked out of the cottage garden, however, it was definitely not singing any longer. After my few exploratory incisions and amputations, it was drooping miserably.

"You probably pulled up the last example of a rare species of some exquisite flower hitherto thought extinct," smiled my husband that evening, as he observed the remains of this autopsied plant on the flagstones.

"I know what we can call your farm," he offered—it was always "his" garden and "my" farm. "Farmageddon. The ultimate battleground."

My husband had become an avid gardener since we moved

out of the city into the suburbs. He happily spent spring and summer weekends relocating heavy clumps of perennials to "definitely sunnier spots," and then relocating them once again as the shadows shifted. He loved to follow the directions on seed packets, to rake our clay soil into a beautiful pebbly grain (until the first rain), to fertilize and exhort and transplant and prune ad nauseam—ad meam nauseam. And it has been a complementary relationship over the years, with my enthusiasm for his well-staked tomatoes which he insists he plants only for me, and his happy solitude digging craters to shelter his cucumber sproutings.

"I love planting," he said one day. "Planting is like setting a little time bomb. You poke a seed in the ground. You forget about it. And then later, boom!"

There was only one year, when my husband broke his leg, that I was entrusted with the spring planting of the garden—his garden. In the evenings during the course of those three months, he and I would head outside with trowel, seeds, hose, and a stool. I pushed everything along in the wheelbarrow, solemnly hanging my head and giving the procession something of a funereal air. My husband would orchestrate the garden blueprint from his stool, gesturing with a crutch, while I drew a finger through the dirt to make a row for coriander and poked cucumber seeds down one inch or so. The experience brought me face to face with that hoard of deep-threaded anxieties about the delicate and unpredictable nature of plants, their noiseless lives. The days I spent waiting for signs of life from the watered soil seemed interminable. And once the plants broke surface, a series of hazards seemed to await them. There were the rabbits, deer, and woodchucks. There was, among the calendulas and tomatoes, a "five-o'clock wilt" after a day of unmitigated sunshine—it was enough to ruin my dinner. And when the arugula bolted at only four inches of height, and microscopic white worms were gainfully goring every red radish we had, I was convinced that I, as a gardener, was not Mother Nature's torch bearer.

"Oh, how satisfying this geranium bed is," cooed my neighbor one morning from across her white picket fence. She was rosily lopping off the browning blossoms and throwing Miracle Gro over the lot. "Shall I come over and help you weed?"

Weed? I thought. Which one is the weed? I looked up at her with a pair of industrial-scale vine shears dangling from my hand. She had clearly construed that my husband's beloved pole beans faced a greater peril from my hand than from the multiplicity of slugs and beetles that supped on them. So she walked over and nestled herself between the Bibb lettuce and the basil and started pinching out the aggressive threads of new grass and clover.

"This is your lettuce." She pointed. "And this is just a weed." She held up something very healthy-looking, and smiled. "You say you're in agriculture?"

I was indeed "in agriculture," I supposed. After studying agricultural economics at Texas A&M University, I had gone on to work first for a cattle genetics company, then for a grain export company, and later for a specialty beef company. These were corporate encounters of the agribusiness kind, but I think they contributed something to my interest in small-scale farming. They kept my thoughts trained on animal breeds, corn prices, and industry issues, and they kept my ear tuned to the field and to the vocabulary of farming. Above all, they made me feel cheerlessly remote from what I had begun to love in agriculture, which was the bread-and-butter of it, the daily chores.

Livestock had been the focus of most of my agribusiness career, and because of that I felt most comfortable with the idea of handling cattle, sheep, poultry, and pigs—well, pigs only if necessary. I daydreamed about proper fencing techniques, about irrigation channels and feed bunks. I subscribed to magazines that kept me updated with tips on handling calves, feeding pregnant goats, and measuring the moisture content of hay in my microwave oven. I wrote to the publishers. I said, How can I keep the flies off my calves, and What if I don't have a microwave oven, which I don't?

Fruit and vegetable crops I had only an indirect sense about, but a commercial instinct, which is why I went to work on area vegetable farms when we moved to Greenwich, and which is also why I tended to bring steel-industry tools to bear upon our little garden out back. I was an unwitting Goliath in that leafy patch. It made me irritable that everything was so petite and that I must surely have seemed more a menace to my husband's vegetables than an aide.

Yes, I'm in agriculture, I would fume to myself. I sit behind a desk each day and imagine supertankers full of soybeans and frozen pork bellies crisscrossing the globe.

The real roots of my decision to have a farm originated before my agribusiness involvement. I look back to childhood and childhood friends, to a semester off from college when I worked on a cattle ranch in Wyoming, to my unwavering interest in natural resources and to my long-standing and undernourished love of livestock. These experiences together introduced me to the multiple facets of agrarian life. These were the roots of my desire to farm, the roots of that plant I came across.

·

I grew up in the town of Northampton, Massachusetts, at a time when it was still a small college town tucked into the foothills of the Berkshire mountains and ringed by small farms of cucumbers, asparagus, corn, and tobacco. My family lived at the edge of Smith College, the oldest women's college in the country. The campus was lovely, full of green fields, gardens, huge brick and clapboard houses that served as dormitories, and a pond on which the whole town skated out its winters.

Our own home was a big yellow house just beyond a brick quadrangle of student dormitories. It was an old three-storey house that had originally been built to accommodate wealthy patricians during their recuperation from treatments at the local hospital. That was in the day when Harrison Avenue was fields and meadows. It is now a thoroughly residential street, replete with a creative variety of neighbors that bring the issues of the world literally to one's doorstep—AIDS, divorce, yuppies, affairs, even the superbly restrained vendettas waged over swimming pools, backyard fences, and aerial antennas.

My parents moved to Northampton in 1957. My father was for many years the only local psychoanalyst for the area colleges and the community at large. Psychoanalysts were a rare commodity in the 1950s. Like cancer or divorce, their work was a subject one didn't discuss. It's hard to imagine that reserve nowadays, as we have evolved into such an all-baring, long-winded culture for whom cancer, divorce, and psychotherapy are mundane and chat-worthy issues. My father suffered a further image problem by refusing to identify himself with "the Freudians" or "the Jungians," a choice that denied people a quick and comfortable laying on of pigeonholing hands. He would say that human beings are too varied to have a simple set of methodologies applied to them, that you must take each person as he or she is, complicated and conflicted.

Since the very first mention of my agricultural aspirations, my father has been delighted by the idea of a farm in the family. He remembers sharing a bivouac in World War II with a farmer from Indiana, an "extremely decent man," he recalled, with enormous and strong hands. "Look at your hands," he had said to the soldier. "You've got hands the size of a ham. And your wrists!"

My mother graduated from Smith College in 1948. She had loved the town and the college, and their images were to recur quietly and fondly in her books. Words were her métier, as a critic and novelist. She taught herself French by reading Proust, and she wanted her children to be avid readers. We all did grow to be readers and writers, although my own start was relatively sluggish. When I was in my teens, my mother was still devising inventive bribes for me to "just get through" a smattering of pages of Galsworthy per month. Even now I cannot pick up a Galsworthy novel without distress, because he has remained synonymous for me with a torturous ennui—and my failure to overcome it.

After years of treatments and remissions, my mother died of Hodgkin's disease when I was a senior in college. I was too late to tell her a lot of things. Death, I think, is an ongoing lesson in finality, and so I have had to come to grips, periodically, with The Next Thing I will not be able to tell her. She would not have guessed about the farm, though it was she who spent the summers of her own childhood breathing in the white dandruff air from the duck farms of East Moriches, Long Island, and she, I think, who had good instincts about handling all kinds of creatures that crossed her path.

My one brother, the eldest child in the family, left the house quickly and angrily in the mid-1960s. My three older sisters— a doctor, a lawyer, and an art conservator—were more vividly a part of my own growing up. I watched them mature, I attended their high school honor roll initiations, I helped to move their plants and record albums into their college dorm rooms, and I missed them when my own time came for these rites. What will they all think of the farm, I wonder. And I'm quite sure they'll let me know.

There was a lot of Ivy in my family, and Ivy became a kind of premise for me, too, although I advanced to it in many respects blithely unaware. I was an average student, "mediocre," as my high school English teacher once verified for me in her singeing way. Still, the powers of the public school system posited me in various accelerated programs along the way—a choice, I was sure, that rested on my trailing so much Phi Beta Kappa material in the form of my sisters. As early as the fourth grade, I was bused to a special classroom that seemed leagues away from home (probably two miles), and it was there that I met Barbara, a Polish girl whose family lived behind the county fairgrounds on a farm. I loved to go over to her home, a modest olive-green two-storey house which she shared with her mother (a hairdresser), a blind and markedly homely sister who, in the throes of her own private agonies, demeaned and bullied Barbara, and a grandmother and grandfather who milked the twelve dairy cows and tilled the acreage in corn. Only Barbara and her sister spoke English as a first language. Her mother stammered by to confer on hair lengths and groceries, but her grandparents spoke no English at all.

In Barbara's house, I was acquainted with exotic dishes like golumpki, pirogi, and tomatoes in sour cream. We played in the barns, and would squat quietly in the hay beside her grandfather as he milked his cows by hand. I was suffered on occasion to feel the hot flanks and udders of the cows and to try my own hand at squeezing a teat. Barbara's grandfather thought that the finest gift a child could be given was a glass of warm, fresh milk. In fact, most people will agree that warm milk, straight from the udder, is a taste acquired only by dint of strenuous conviction. Unstrained, unchilled, unseparated milk enamors one only of machine-sure filtration and homogenization. The warm cup that Barbara's grandfather would extend to me—he grinning the proud and toothless grin of a European peasant farmer, me with eyes wide and lower lip quivering—seemed like an initiation by fire. Well, and it made me feel very, very mature to put down that milk without tears. At the time I viewed it as a fair price to pay for staying overnight at the farm.

During the winters, when my mother would drive me over to Barbara's house, we would turn off one rubbly gravel road onto the frozen, rutted earth of the barnyard driveway. Three foaming and barking German shepherd guard dogs invariably jumped to alarm. They would strain forward with their teeth bared, their necks defying imminent severance by their collars, only a skimpy chain hampering them from reaching us. From eating us, we agreed. We would wait in the car until Barbara or her mother came to rescue me, and to usher me, shivering, into the house. Then my mother, shivering also, would drive home.

On such days, Barbara and I would go for walks in the half-frozen mud of the barnyard, where tractor ruts were covered with a thin sheet of ice, hiding pools of yellow-green cow urine that seemed never to disappear. We would walk into the fields, Barbara in a heavy sweater, I stumbling beside her in an awkward, bulky, and completely incapacitating orb of a snowsuit, hobbling over the snow and the blond stubble of hay poking up through it. We would visit the cows and avoid with a fuss the yellow snow they left about them. We would watch a pile of fresh manure melt an aureole about itself and show the grass bright green beneath.

Northampton was surrounded by small farms like that of Barbara's family. I have heard that the alluvial soil of the Connecticut River Valley, its loess, is some of the finest soil in the country. In the summers, many of my school friends would work for the valley farms. Some picked cucumbers and corn. Most picked tobacco under the gauzy, cream-colored nets, and hung the leaves to dry in the familiar long red barns whose vertical slats were opened in the summer for aeration. Massachusetts and Connecticut still host the largest number of cigar wrapper and cigar binder tobacco leaf growers in the nation, but their netted fields, marked by steepling red and black barns and once such a common piece of the landscape, now must be sought out with the aid of guidebooks. Highways and housing developments roll over many of the old tobacco farms, the developments having adopted names like Valley Farms, Silo Circle, or Tobacco Hill.

Northampton evolved over the years into a bustling nucleus of boutiques and bistros, wealthy young parents, and enormous malls, each with the same clothing stores and organic food markets. Gradually the town attracted an increasing number of lesbians and became known as a kind of East Coast capital for women who preferred women and preferred to let you know. The J. J. Newberry's and the McCallum's disappeared and instead you could buy Italian shoes, French unfitted sheets, and blackened redfish, lump fish, or catfish. Psychotherapists now hang their shingles along Main Street, Center Street, and all the side streets as well—so many therapists, it seems, that there is simply no excuse for staying troubled in Northampton.

I went back to Northampton last summer to visit the local Agway dealership in town. Agway is a Northeast cooperative that has spent the last few decades being bought and sold and bought again. The exodus of farming from this region of the country has taken a severe toll on businesses like Agway that supplied equipment, feeds, vehicles, and other production materials to the now-retired small-scale farms.

In Northampton, the Agway store on King Street had somehow managed to survive the town's doggedly insistent adornments of sophistication. When I drove into the Agway parking lot, I began to understand. "Somehow" may have had to do with the fact that the store was currently more apt to be selling snowblowers, birdhouses, and Holland bulbs than, say, chicken feed, pig vaccines, and $150,000 John Deere tractors.

"Feed?" said the woman behind the raised garrison of a four-sided checkout counter.

"Yes."

"Well, honey, I can give you dog feed, cat feed, and bird feed, but we don't sell no—what did you say? *Livestock* feed?"

I walked by shelves of garden spades, bird feeders, green twine, and barbecue grills.

"Seed?" she looked at me like she hadn't heard right.

"Yes."

"I've got *bird* seed, flower seed, and a few packets left of lettuce seed. How much corn were you wanting to grow?"

So I wandered outside onto their tarmac of swing sets, woodchippers, tractor lawn mowers, and wilting flats of unidentifiable blossomless flowers.

"*Tractor* tractors?" she was sighing now.

"Yes."

"Not a lawn mower?"

"No."

"Oh, honey. I think we're three for three for you today. But look here. Here's a catalogue. Anything in it you like, I'm sure we can order for you."

She heaved toward me a ponderous graying lump of an out-of-date Agway sales catalogue. I thanked her for her trouble and went to my car to regroup.

•

In my family, extraordinary emphasis was laid on semantics. We often discussed the appropriateness of specific words, the connotations and denotations of words, what words meant to a novelist or to a psychoanalyst or the fellow on his couch. One of the points that my father most stressed was how word use could define a person's sense of self. For example, he once explained to me, it's one thing if you say a person is alcoholic, but if you say he or she is *an* alcoholic—if you turn the adjective into a noun—you essentially trap and curtail that person's identity.

"People too often get named, or identified, by their symptoms," he would say. Words like *homosexual* or *alcoholic* were really descriptive adjectives instead of comprehensively identifying nouns.

"I suppose it's almost like using a synecdoche," my father said, "where you're identifying a whole association of things by one aspect." Evocative in poetry, he added, but it rarely did justice to a whole, complex human being.

So when I decided to start a farm, I couldn't help but ruminate on the question: What was the difference between being a farmer and farming? What were the connotations of being a farmer, and did I like them? I knew that my husband had contended with similar questions. He would bristle when called a banker

—which indeed he was for all conventional purposes—because he didn't like the connotations. He often preferred the nebulous phrase "I work in finance." Verbs are much more freeing than nouns.

One day a friend sent me a poem that had been published in *Harvard Magazine*. The little biographical blurb at the bottom of the page said the poet was a blueberry farmer in Maine. It made me recoil. The image seemed at once pretentious and overly coy. I wasn't put in mind of the plain hard work and bird-battling of blueberry farming; rather I caught myself connecting the words with a kind of dainty, flowery self-avowal. It wasn't a rational attribution. I knew very well how strenuous farming is. Maybe it was just the blueberries, alliterative and adorable, that seemed to ally themselves these days more with ginghams and dolls than with farmers' woes and pails.

The incident made me realize that in many ways I was bashful about the idea of calling myself a farmer. I didn't want to be identified with cute crops. I would rather have planted one of those merciless fields of cotton, I thought, than be affiliated with a farm with a corny image. You're a snob, I said to myself, and I was right. I would have bent over backward to adhere to the image of a peasant laborer before I let myself look the part of a beribboned daisy-picker. Unnerved to discover these intransigent feelings in myself, I wondered if other people felt the same way about farming and the connotations of "being a farmer." I sought out the opinions of family and friends.

"I'm going to start a farm," I would say, testing the waters. And there was a broad gamut of response.

"Adorable. When do we eat?"

"Upwind or downwind of me?"

"Do farms have posts and lintels or only ranches?"

"Wonderful," said one friend. "A good idea tastes like honey, doesn't it?"

"Mankind has struggled for centuries to release himself from that drudgery," commented another.

"You're going to kill baby sheep?"

"A fine tradition."

There's nothing like a fine tradition, I decided. But it's even better when one knows a little something about what that tradition is. It being a Sunday evening, I picked up, with interest and irony, the Bible.

According to the Old Testament, food came before agriculture in the scheme of things. In Genesis 1, God created seafood and poultry on the fifth day. Beef, bugs, salad, and fruit arrived on day six, which was fortuitous for Adam and Eve, because they also came into being that morning or afternoon.

And God said to everybody (1:22; 1:28): "Be fruitful and multiply." But to man, he added: ". . . and fill the earth and subdue it; and have dominion over the fish of the sea and over the birds of the air and over every living thing that moves upon the earth."

He went on (1:29): "Behold, I have given you every plant yielding seed which is upon the face of all the earth, and every tree with seed in its fruit; you shall have them for food." And for all of the other creatures, God provided "every green plant for food" (1:30).

Genesis 2, however, presents a slightly different chronology. Here, man appears "formed . . . of dust from the ground," after earth was watered, but before it was planted. So from this version, only after "man became a living being" did God create "a garden in Eden, in the east; and there he put the man whom he had formed. And out of the ground the Lord God made to grow every tree that is pleasant to the sight and good for food . . ."

And then (2:15): "The Lord God took the man and put him in the Garden of Eden to till it and keep it." This is the first implication that food is going to take some cultivation by Adam and his helper, Eve; but, or so it would seem by all accounts, the Garden required very low maintenance indeed.

With the expulsion from Eden, God condemned Adam to the

exertions of farming. "Cursed is the ground because of you," he said; "in toil you shall eat of it all the days of your life; thorns and thistles it shall bring forth to you; and you shall eat the plants of the field. In the sweat of your face you shall eat bread till you return to the ground, for out of it you were taken; you are dust, and to dust you shall return" (3:17–19).

Outside the Garden of Eden, food was going to be a function of man's willingness to labor. Abel became a shepherd and Cain became a farmer, among other things. And the Bible would have you believe it all went downhill from there.

There are lots of versions of agricultural Beginnings, and some greet the science of agriculture more as a blessing than as a punishment. For the ancient Egyptians, it was the wise and powerful god Osiris who taught men to farm—giving them a tidier and more reliable alternative to foraging and cannibalism. In Greek mythology, Demeter was goddess of the cornfield. She ministered not only the sowing of farm crops and the breeding of animals, but also the matrimonial bed, where mankind's corresponding seeds and eggs were, one infers, of nearly comparable importance. When Demeter learned that it was Hades who had carried off her daughter, Persephone, she cast a scourge upon the earth. As Robert Graves wrote in *the Greek Myths,* volume I: "Demeter was so angry that, instead of returning to Olympus, she continued to wander about the earth, forbidding the trees to yield fruit and the herbs to grow, until the race of men stood in danger of extinction." But after Persephone was restored to her for the larger part of each year, Demeter sent one of her priests to earth to resurrect the parched ground. "Triptolemus she supplied with seed-corn, a wooden plough, and a chariot drawn by serpents; and sent him all over the world to teach mankind the art of agriculture." When the Romans embraced the gods of the Greeks, they called Demeter's counterpart Ceres, from which name is derived the word *cereal.*

As I decided to start a farm, the mythologies of the "original farmer" became mine to investigate, just as we all negotiate our personal images within the context of images set forth by our family and culture. But it was no mere exercise in introspection—modern farming has not extricated itself wholly from ancient teachings and rituals. You can still trace the force of early religious and folklorish edict in some cultures' farming practices today. Plenty of farmers swear that one must sow upward-growing plants such as pole beans when the moon is waxing, and downward-growing plants like carrots when the moon is waning. We have visited Shaker, Amish, and Mennonite villages where antiquated farming customs are preserved. Also maintained over time were the revered, millennia-old dietary laws of the Old Testament, the Kashruth. Kashruth dictates the way kosher food must be prepared and eaten among observant Jews even today.

Whenever I have worked on farms, I have found my thoughts drifting back to the early agricultural parables, perhaps because the very nature of manual work leaves one's mind open to unhampered thinking, and perhaps because many basic farm chores today are remarkably unremoved from farm chores thousands of years old—shoveling out irrigation canals and mounding dikes, milking cows or collecting seed. Frequently my thoughts idle on the polarity between cultures whose mythologies teach that their seminal founders somehow fell from grace and were condemned to agricultural toil, and those whose lore holds that their people were honored and rewarded by the gift of agricultural knowledge. It's part of a dialectical litany in agriculture between the peasant laborer and the champion provider. Do we perceive agriculture as a chore and the burdensome province of the poorest tier of the laity, or do we see agriculture as a wisdom and the blessed inheritance of mankind? In fact, it is a little of both, as is true with most of life. Farming encompasses both the tedium of manual labor and the richness of the most elaborate science.

Then, taking the idea a step further: Might this discrepancy in founding mythologies persist through time to have any bearing on our culture's contemporary attitudes toward its agricultural sector? Suppose the original farmer really had been the fruit of a divinely convicted and penalized parentage? How else might this farmer have evolved over time, conceptually, but as the lower class, the sweated peasantry, the peon? Around him, then, the other levels of maturing civilization—the royalty, the bourgeoisie, the burghers—would be seated higher on the social ladder for not having to produce their own foodstuffs. And arranged on the rungs of a comfortably distinct ladder would be the clergy, God's servants, who would sometimes farm, sometimes procure. Historically, of course, they had their own internal hierarchies, their own sense of what, exactly, was God's work. It was typically the local proletariat who pruned the monastery orchards, for there were, after all, a lot of manuscripts to copy.

But suppose the original farmer had instead been conceived of as the fortunate heir to sacred agricultural knowledge. I had some difficulty in seeing that positive image sustaining itself over time. It could be that, ten or so thousand years ago, when the first primitive communities of the Middle East's Fertile Crescent (not recognizable today, hardly fertile, a desert of war debris) were catching on to the reproductive capacities of their grains, individuals who flaunted a green thumb were celebrated by the others of that community. The better farmers may even have been tribal chiefs of a sort—we don't know. However, by the time our informative stone tablets became clearer a few millennia later, it seemed that farmers were not ascending to the upper echelons of civic hierarchy. Wealth and power were already attaching to ownership of fertile land, but the actual exertions of farming had been relegated by and large to the lower castes, the slaves of the king or the local peasantry.

The myth of a divinely favored farmer would appear to have lost steam over the course of time, in part, I believe, because agriculture necessarily became a communal chore and not the divine calling of a few heroic individuals; and then especially in the face of farming's intrinsic grind, which is hard to dispute. All in all, I think that the instinctive ascent of civilization, with its secular structural efficiencies and its growth, organized or chaotic, has always tended to subsume the farmer's stature into some necessary, primary, and highly strenuous constituent of society. This last bit—the highly strenuous part—would naturally have impelled the more powerful segments of society to elude such a role. Farming, when possible, would be relegated, not extolled.

If I did become a farmer, I knew there would be people who would view me as someone who was without a more enlightened choice, someone to whom the food-raising chores of society were relegated. I, rather, take a divergent view and keen comfort in the agreeable image of the gentleman farmer, which surfaces periodically in our agrarian legacy. The image of the gentleman farmer recalls most precisely for me the aristocratic agriculturalists of the nineteenth century, but the concept might be used even more broadly to describe the wonderfully curious and methodical landowners who have for centuries kept records of their crops and animal husbandry and cleverly experimented with their scant sciences to improve their yields. The gentleman farmer, in my mind, is a character from a sort of secular myth —one in which elegant sciences fit comfortably alongside commonplace chores.

When I reflect on the way the complex dimensions of agricultural mythologies have sustained their lessons by word of mouth or monastery, mingled and expressed (or not) through successive centuries, I'm reminded of the way human genes are passed on, mingled and expressed (or not) through generations of families. This parallel, like a barge, carries me over the river from the propositions of parable to the propositions of biology, and I wonder what Darwinian logic would have to impart with respect to the genesis and evolution of the farmer.

In evolutionary theory, food evolved simultaneously with every tapeworm and brontosaurus. In fact, the same worm and dinosaur *became* someone else's food when their days or hours of eating were over. All evolutionary organisms spent their limited time and energies rummaging the earth's terrestrial and aquatic regions for food. Even plant life forages the air and soil for desirable gasses and nutrients as they fumble by. All the time.

For the early dedicated herbivores there was a gamut of plant life to satisfy appetites, from the tiniest algae to large, leafy shrubs. Sauropods, believed to have been the largest of the herbivorous dinosaurs (the small-headed, long-necked, round-bodied, copacetic chewers of greens, invariably portrayed in the movies as friendly types), were equipped with a sorely lacking dental set for eating the upwards of three hundred pounds of greens they are supposed to have needed each day.

For the carnivores, the basic rules of the hunt applied. Larger animals ate smaller animals. Quicker animals ate slower animals. Smarter animals ate dumber animals, and this is where many optimists think man got his leg up on the game. Today, of course, there is some sensible reluctance toward accepting the hypothesis that man is more advanced than other creatures. There is also a scaling aversion to his continued habit of eating the "dumber" others.

Eating, and hoping to do so again soon, made up the daily life of the earth's primordial creatures. Food meant survival, and survival favored the most fit of species and specimens. But food was not always easy to come by. Weather, competitors, natural scarcities, and spoilage were some of the impediments to a regular meal. This kept most animals, human and otherwise, on the move, seeking out an achievable prey or familiar plants. Hunting was a high-risk occupation no matter where you stood on the food chain, and gathering was no picnic either. When man learned how to farm, he took the revolutionary step of subduing a tremendous entropy in his existence. By cultivating crops, he tamed the haphazard nature of his food supply. He could settle down, shed the nomadic life. By the same token, he could move—take his seeds and expertise to better soils or more clement weathers. It was in this way that agriculture allowed civilizations to take root and to spread.

Whether divinely bestowed or intellectually ferreted out, agriculture has always meant the subjugation of the soil and select species for the creation of foodstuff for mankind. People who believed their god(s) was (were) responsible for this prayed gratefully through the centuries for a continued bounty. They offered to their heavens a share of the harvest—some organs from the ox, a fetus from the llama, or a bowl of fruit—to say thank you, and please keep up the good work. Other peoples have no doubt cursed those same heavens for withholding rain or sending locusts when farming already seemed arduous and profane enough. Whatever the era or locale, it is all the same agriculture, the same exploitation, cultivation, and deployment of the local natural resources toward the ongoing and increasing production of food. Human beings do it. Ants do it, too.

2

Agriculture versus Food

A bumper sticker that came out sometime in the 1960s read: IF YOU EAT FOOD, YOU'RE INVOLVED WITH AGRICULTURE. The objective was to raise the consciousness of Americans about the safety and quality of our food supplies. We had, it was suggested, become too complacent.

As I stride toward becoming a farmer myself, I think about this phrase in reverse: In essence, if you're involved with agriculture, you're involved with food. It may seem obvious, but many agricultural industries have until recently been quite removed from the food issue. They have concerned themselves with a specialized form of sorghum for processing, tomatoes for ketchup, or piglets without stress. When I reflect on the farmers I have known or known of—whether they have raised wheat or beef cattle—I would have to argue that they are not particularly sensitive diners themselves, even though they grow the raw materials.

"I don't understand these farmers I deal with," said a grain buyer and trader I met. "Here they are in North Dakota, say, heartland of America, finest producers of wheat in the world—and what do they eat out there? Junk! Wonder Bread. Canned vegetables. Canned fruit. Canned spaghetti. I say to them, 'Do you know that New Yorkers pay a fortune to eat itsy-bitsy whole grain buns with thick crusts made from *your* wheat, while you eat nothing but pasty white Fluffernutter loaves of puffed flour?' "

When I was working on a cattle ranch in Wyoming during time off from college, I came across the same (dis)respect for diet; steak sauce, Tang, imitation maple syrup, and canned peas and carrots were the staples that sat out on our cookhouse counter. Jelly on white bread was a special favorite among the hands.

The fact is, farmers don't generally go into farming because of their acute dietary discrimination. After harvesting five hundred acres of durum wheat, they don't go to the supermarket to compare quality among various brands of dry noodles. And when I envision establishing a farm, I'm not fantasizing about improving the culinary repertoire of my community—I'm thinking mainly about farming, about sourcing feeds and seeds, about sunny days and soft rains, about wool and meat and onions and so on. Still, I'm aware that if I try to sell lousy produce each year, then I'll lose my customers, lose my business. Basically, whatever I raise I would like to raise the best. So there is a voice inside me steering me toward the tenderest rack of lamb and the sweetest parsnips (the parsnips are for my father; I don't know another person who raves about them). I suspect that it is usually the smaller farm, such as the one I imagine having, that is inclined to cater to consumers' taste buds and strive for overall excellence, because larger, industrial-scale farms have to play the average. The huge commercial farms are founded on principles of bulk, volume, and the processing equipment of their wholesale buyers. They cannot pamper and primp their stock or spinach as might a small boutique farm or even a well-managed medium-size farm—the proverbial family farm. This may be one reason why we Americans have so embraced the idea of our small and family farms: we feel they respond to us, care about our food wants.

In 1988, I watched Representative Richard Gephardt, a Democratic Congressman from Missouri, the Show-Me State, show Americans how fine indeed was the country's sentimental attachment to its "family farmer." He ran for the office of president that year as a strong proponent of the political effort to "save the family farm." The legislation supporting this effort was intended to allocate the bulk of USDA crop subsidies and other like program payments to midsize farms—family farms, which have been gradually squeezed out of business by industrial-size farms and their inherent economies of scale. Family farms are a part of the American heritage, the Gephardt people told us.

But we showed Richard Gephardt that, even though we cared about the family farm idea, we didn't care enough. We enjoyed the low food prices that derived from the relatively low costs enjoyed by the very large-scale farms in this country. And so while we were tugged at by the thought of losing more family farms, we indicated to Mr. Gephardt, through an overall lack of support of his candidacy, that we wished to continue being rather pragmatic about our food production.

In fact, Americans are not pragmatic about our food production at all; we are extraordinarily conflicted about it. The very term *food production* puts a lot of people ill at ease. Most Americans, it would seem, prefer to see food production as two separate and discrete concepts: food and agriculture. Food, people like to know about, talk about, fuss with, fret over, indulge in, do without, and find cheap and without bruises. Agriculture, to the ninety-eight or so percent of Americans who are not farmers, is a discomfiting subject.

People who like to talk about food often don't like to think about agriculture. "Mention agriculture to my editor," said a woman who writes about food for *The New York Times*, "and he begins to hyperventilate." And when food-prepossessed people do turn their glances toward the silo, they frequently assume quite horrified and self-righteous poses vis-à-vis today's accepted practices for raising crops and livestock.

"I will not touch white veal anymore!"

"I heard about chickens! We're only eating fish now."

"Do you know what happens to bananas en route?"

It's difficult to blame them. Farmers have lost touch with consumers in a world where the raising of wheat and cattle is so far removed from the selling of the bread loaf and the steak. And consumers have wallowed collusively in their ignorance about the country's food production systems. It came as something of a surprise in the 1970s when we heard inklings that white veal was the result of overtly inhumane livestock husbandry practices. We were introduced to photographs of calves that mournfully lived out their mere six months in dark crates. We learned that all of those man-made crop-enriching and crop-protecting nutrients were washing into rivers and decimating marine life. And the Europeans broke into our passive daze by firmly declaring that, whether or not steroid growth promotants used in livestock operations deleteriously affected the meat yielded in those operations—*whether or not*—they didn't want that meat anymore.

Clearly, American consumers' long-standing disregard of our agriculture has borne its unsavory results (the Chickens-Come-Home-To-Roost Department). The cheap, bountiful foodstuffs that our presidential candidates have loved to stump about finally came out of the closet and suddenly our images of amber waves of grain were thrust aside. Midwestern topsoil, it seemed, was washing into rivers at a rate of hundreds of tons a day, the barren deserts of Southern California had metamorphosed into a prolific kitchen garden for the country, and the farm-chemicals egg had hatched into a broad-winged, tenaciously clawed bird.

So consumers balked—a little. We launched one counter-skirmish against the American farmer by rekindling our flirtation with the organic food industry. It came at the end of the 1980s, spurred on, I think, by our society's growing affluence and its presiding obsession with intake. But, interestingly, the rejuvenated alliance with organics was a brief one, swiftly engulfed in a deluge of mass-market foods, newly advertised as healthy and environmentally-friendly. The Campbell's soup kids slimmed down, and the plump Pillsbury Doughboy seemed temporarily whisked away to the Gulag. Green and beige began to appear on food labels everywhere, and this packaging gimmick, which pretended to some kind of certification from the Sierra Club, seemed to saturate even nonorganic food shelves. Sales of genuine organics crested after a brief missile launch into vogue.

American consumers! We're impossible. We want cheap food, unblemished food, organic food, and noncaloric dessert food. On Sunday afternoons, we want the family farm and the roadside vegetable stand manned by nice folk who do it all for pleasure. And on Monday mornings we sweep imperiously down our supermarket aisles, squarely eschewing nature's irregularities when it comes to the size and shape of our lettuce heads. We're known to rage upon discovering a seed in a navel orange. Hasn't somebody solved that problem yet? we snarl, for we are still feeling irritable about the milk carton's mere two-week shelf life and the way our bagged carrots, like our tomatoes, look the proper color and shape but taste routinely like shirt cardboards. Americans prefer to imagine that our farmers, like our doctors, work in an arena of perfect, mathematical science, an arena where outcomes are predictable and results consistent. But in fact farmers, just like doctors, operate on live genetic material and confront the vagaries of a complex, respiring code. Sometimes there will still be seeds in a navel orange, but they're working on it.

·

I saw the conflict between food and farming firsthand one year when I worked on a small vegetable farm in New England. It was composed of a hundred acres, mostly scenic hilltop, now locked in by country clubs, capacious estates, and horse-riding rings. The land was farmed by a seventy-year-old man and his son, Richie. And Richie was agitated and angry with his lot.

"Name a golf course in this county," he would growl to me.

"We used to farm it." It was Richie who eventually repainted the sign at the farm's front gate to read, LUCCO'S FARM: THIS IS *NOT* AN ORGANIC FARM.

"These New Yorkers," he would complain to me, "come up on the weekend and roll down our field road, real slow, real careful, in their fancy German cars. They wanna pick strawberries. They wanna pick out their own head of lettuce. They bring the kids. They bring the dog. They trample around the berries for a few minutes and then they ask about discounts. I say to them, 'I don't give discounts.' They tell me about their grandmother's senior citizen card—she's been sitting in the back seat of the car this whole time with the air conditioning turned up. And then they ask me why don't I go organic. 'You're probably right,' I say to them. 'Now I got work to do.' Me, without a fancy car, with two kids, just trying to make ends meet, you know? I wanna say, 'The only thing to put me outa business faster than wimpy scabby bruised-up organic produce is people like you.' "

Richie ran one of the last pick-your-own diversified vegetable farms in the region. He operated this way because he figured he came out ahead through lower labor costs, but most of his farmer friends had stopped letting people onto their farms at all.

"John, Johnny B., Frank, and Mario," Richie used to grumble, "they all go wholesale only now. They think I'm crazy to let people on the farm. One old lady trips between the rows and I'm a goner, they say. But you know, I like that folks like to come here. They think I'm happier than them for doing this, and maybe I am. I dunno. Maybe I'm just crazy. But don't forget, I grow the biggest damn beets in New England."

People did indeed like driving down the pitted dirt road to Richie's corrugated iron lean-to shed. They would park under an enormous old maple tree that was industriously toppling the shed with its slow and steady root growth. They did indeed enjoy trampling Richie's strawberry plants in search of the one perfect red orb. And most of all they loved to tell us—the farm hands—how great it felt to be "in touch with actual food." They would stand at the scales for ten or fifteen minutes, eating their berries before we weighed them and chatting with us about their feelings of disenfranchisement from food nowadays.

"This is wonderful," they would say. "You may not realize it, young lady, but you are very very fortunate to be working here."

"I'm going to bring my children back tomorrow," said one woman. "I want to show them what real food is. They honestly think supermarkets make food."

I could only smile. I understood what they were feeling. Visitors to the farm were so heartened to find produce without cellophane wrapping that they immediately ascribed to our vegetables a hoard of other delightful attributes—a healthier tinge, better flavor, nicer leaves. Spinach from the supermarket, they would grimace to me confidentially, well it just didn't taste like much of anything.

"Be sure to wash or rinse everything," I would say to the people who came by. Even though I rank among the worst offenders of this policy, I encourage others to believe in it. Richie's farm chemicals notwithstanding, the world is full of bacteria, and the schmoozing bugs and deer and rabbits that customarily gambol through farm fields are notorious carriers of filth and disease. A few omissions to the washing rule are not harmful, and there is no need to go overboard by boiling every tomato and pear you buy, but from my own background in farming I have learned to wash rigorously after leaving the barn or fields—wash both myself and Richie's green peppers.

As for Richie's customers, I agreed with them about the satisfaction of seeing vegetables in the soil. Children were invariably thrilled to find plump crescents of pea pods dangling under the thick shade of green vine and tendrils. The youngest, especially, seemed to know next to nothing about the origins of their food. Most mothers I chatted with spoke resolutely about their intentions to teach their kids how chocolate milk is produced or

french fries raised, although they usually had a clause about meat.
"No," they would say, fidgety. "I don't think Stevie has to
learn where his hamburger patties come from yet."

To be fair, I never rolled my eyes until after I (or they) had
walked away. Furthermore, it wasn't that I expected infants to
understand the horror of animal slaughter, but that, of the few
terms in the English language that I abhor, *patty* is one—*hamburger patty* is another. As for knowing where your meat comes
from, that's a delicate theme, and I have nothing against leaving
children in the dark for years.

When I was a child, there was always a butcher stationed in
the meat section of our local A&P. Aproned and stout, he was
usually to be found out front by the beef case, rearranging heavy
packs of hamburger and steaks. In those days beef, if it was
prized, was so fatty and marbled that it tended to look a pale
pink, not purple or red. Our butcher loved to fuss with the
steaks until he found one he felt you truly deserved—the premium cuts, laced with yellowish veins of fat that certified the
animal had been richly corn-fed. And when he was through
reshuffling these packs of manna, he went back behind a big
plate-glass window to his cutting room, where he would set to
carving hunks of this prime beef off a massive hindquarter or
forequarter. I could see the shiny metal hooks that ran on a rail
along the ceiling of the bright white room, more than one
weighted down by a carcass quarter in reserve; and I could see
blood. I used to bend way over at the waist and twist my neck
up to look at the hindquarters upside-down. Since they were
hung from their hocks on the rails, I could from this angle try
to imagine the full reconstruction of a real cow from these
massive, detached contours of legs-plus of bone, steak, and fat.
No sir, it certainly didn't look like any cow I'd ever seen. And
the Northampton A&P was certainly no showcase for bloodied
heads, hooves, and testicles also triumphantly displayed for sale,
letting you know this was once indeed the cow you'd known.
I had seen that as a child in France, where the butchers wore

bloodied aprons with pride. The French were savages. They ate snails, even. *Our* cows were happy.

So I dangled my head happily upside-down by the meat case while the white-frocked butcher trimmed a roast for seven. Then, just before I went down from vertigo: "Come on now, grocery stores aren't playgrounds." That would be my mother. Off we would go to the next aisle of adventure.

The experience of today's butcher departments has become one of unsullied stainless steel meat cases and white plastic cutting boards (because wood is now considered by the USDA to be too difficult to clean and sterilize). No carcasses are hanging behind the counter, and many bright red steaks are now purple under the vacuum packing, which took place somewhere in Iowa. Moreover, what has happened in the meat case has happened throughout the whole supermarket. When I do the food shopping these days, I'm hardly put in mind of any farmer behind the works. Instead, I'm left to sort through quadruple shelves of uniform breads, identical cookies, and flawless blocks of processed cheese; even some "fresh foods" look like they were born to plastic wrapping.

"I must be from a different epoch," sighed my father one day as we shopped together for dinner ingredients. "This all looks so artificial to me." He was passing a pristine pyramid of shiny Red Delicious apples that seemed jewellike under the tinted lights of the fruit bins. We pushed our cart over to the meat case, where a bright red sign pointed to Perdue's Perfect Chickens.

"Perfection has its alienating side," he said. "A kind of sterility that belongs not to sanitation, but to rebuffing the observer." He advanced toward the lamb section.

"People seem to want their foods that uniform today," I said. "Their cutlets matching, their eggs all the same size, their chicken marigold-yellow. I think a farmer would shoot himself if he heard you complain that his produce looked too perfect."

"You know, I was raised in an era when we were moving as

far away as possible from dirt," my father went on. "In the thirties, people were still very concerned about contamination and food spoilage. There was always a lot of conversation and apprehension about spoilage, and a sharing of tips on how to prevent it. Of course, we didn't have Frigidaires and such when I was a child. It was ice boxes then.

"Nowadays, you don't hear the talk about spoiled food. Well, you've got a salmonella scare for undercooked poultry, I guess. And undercooked fish pose a worry, too, but trichinosis in pork is virtually eliminated, and the nature is completely cooked out of milk these days, and they've learned to line cans so that you can let food sit in them forever. That's a great improvement in terms of sanitation and convenience."

It was interesting to hear my father's ambivalent and, to me, relatively veteran perspective on today's food. I agreed with him about the remarkable degree of safety we enjoy in today's food supply compared with that of several decades ago; but I also agreed that food has a way of looking too perfect these days, and occasionally a bit waxy or plasticky. I sometimes miss that sense of the fragility of fresh food—the fragility that still befalls other plants, like the painted daisies and lupines in my husband's perennial bed.

When my husband and I went on vacation last year, we forgot a bunch of grapes and half a head of iceberg lettuce in the refrigerator for two weeks. Upon our return, I had some trepidation about digging them out—dreading whatever color they might have turned, whatever exotic mold they would be cultivating.

"This is men's work," I said to my husband, and pointed at the refrigerator door.

But they were fine. The grapes were just sitting there, plumpish, juicy, the lettuce still crispy when I bowled it into the garbage pail. That was not a particularly comforting feeling. It was the kind of incident that tempts you to perform laboratory tests. Knowing that fresh lettuce leaves gathered from my husband's garden would wilt in a matter of hours, I was bewildered by these stout and impervious heads that I could find daily in the supermarket. Everyone knew they had already traveled over 2,794 miles (Los Angeles to New York City) cross-country to get here. I felt like I had spun 180 degrees, back to wanting a little silt to wash off my spinach leaves.

If you ask a farmer—and farmers generally visualize food and agriculture as more closely associated than does the general public—he might tell you there was definitely dirt on those spinach leaves when they left his field. After that point, he doesn't know who does what to them. Farmers often sell to distributors, packers, or processing companies that wash, trim, butcher, package, chill, gas, box and otherwise transform raw agricultural produce into neat, inviting bundles of shelf-stable (or pyramid-building) supermarket food. There is a sizable distance between sandy spinach leaves and the washed, chopped, frozen spinach that arrives in 1¼-by-4-by-5¼-inch boxes in the freezer case—and frozen vegetables probably represent the simplest end of the processing sequence. You're really a far cry from the farmer when you eat those frozen pot pies or canned tamales. You're at the threshold of somebody's laboratory kitchen. Most of today's supermarket foods spend some amount of time in this type of kitchen after they leave the farm.

If you think about it, it's rarely the farmer making pitches to the food shopper anymore. He has conferred that job, that territory, upon those zealous food processing companies that thirst overtly for your dollars all over the nation's billboards and televisions. It is the food companies that create and embellish the food we buy, that roll with the punches of our capricious tastes and fads, that interpret our encoded cash register tapes and reformulate their packages and prices accordingly. It is the food companies that take our trending temperatures and turn around and tell the farmer to raise bigger-framed cattle, leaner hogs, redder peppers, larger grapefruits, and higher-protein wheat. If you're discontented with your food options these days, you have to bring your complaints to the General Foods, the Nabiscos, and the ConAgras—not to the farmer.

Having directed you thus, I confess you may or may not find a willing ear at the other end of the line. Some food companies view the common food shopper and his or her fickle preferences more as an aggravation than as their bread and butter. After all, these food companies had only just perfected their updated Ray Bradbury–style "retort" bags that enabled them to sell *en plein air* shelf-stable, indestructible, microwaveable dinners—a veritable "taking the hill" of the pressed-for-time 1980s—when the public mood whimsically swayed back toward fresh products and recyclable containers. This kind of shift in tastes makes a food company feel, if only temporarily, bamboozled by its Average Food Shopper—"she," as they like to say—who suddenly abandons the crusade for convenience for the morality-rich priorities of the combined food-safety and environmentalist movements. "She" is nowadays more interested in foods with less packaging, fewer additives and preservatives, less salt, less fat, and less sugar, than in those excessively predictable and neatly trayed (and under 200 calories, what with those new vegetable gums) freezer entrées.

Not an easy customer. I suppose that's why there are already some ten different versions of the common Coke. And I imagine I, too, may bump into this mercurial consumer problem one day when I become a farmer. The store manager to whom I sell my lettuces may tell me to bring only the red-leaf variety from now on; he doesn't want my green-leaf heads because his customers don't seem to go for them.

"What's the matter with your customers?" I might wail. And there I would be, driving home that night to ten acres of just-maturing green Romaine leaves. In these scenarios, the store manager acts as a kind of interpreter between the farmer and the consumer. Nowadays, this is the most basic, direct form of the dialogue between farmer and food shopper, unless the farmer can operate his own farm stand—essentially, unless the farmer can be his own retailer.

The gulf between original producer and ultimate consumer is only widening as we Americans eat more and more processed foods. When we choose breakfast cereals or prepared dinners as opposed to, say, my hypothetical red-leaf lettuces, we're thrusting an additional layer of negotiation between ourselves and the farmer. Now it is not just the retailer, but the modern food processor, positioned between the supermarket shelf and the farm furrow, who relays messages back and forth. Understanding this may help to throw light on why food costs what it does, and how the farmer's role in our final food products has so diminished over time.

Few of us relish the notion of processed foods, but we Americans continue to consume them at ever-increasing rates. To many minds, processing connotes food-manhandling, the infusion of dyes and various questionable chemicals, the pulverization and reformulation of foods in such a way as to make them appear unpulverized and unreformulated, and of course, shelf-stable. But food processing actually encompasses a broad range of activities that begin with the simple harvesting of the broccoli or the plucking of the chicken.

"I'm no snob about processed foods," said a friend. "Give me Stouffer's frozen chicken à la king any day. At least I know Stouffer's washed, homogenized, and completely sterilized the stuff. Is it true what they're saying about chickens?"

Almost all raw agricultural products are processed to some extent before we consume them as food. Snapping the tips off green beans is processing them. Boiling oats is a type of processing. My father's barber explained recently that she was preparing sweet and sour pirogi for her husband's parents. Now *that's* food processing—if it isn't food poisoning.

Processing is, essentially, preparing food for eating. A more advanced level of food processing is carried on by the leagues of food technologists and food scientists, a relatively new breed of food engineers who explore even the molecular composition of foods. They talk without emotion about flavor, texture, and content. They design foods from natural and arguably unnatural ingredients. They work in laboratories, wear white coats, and tinker with bottles of clear esters and very unkitchenlike appliances. Apples, in their hands, turn into apple fillings. Pieces of a livestock carcass that we don't even like to think about are transformed on their counters into meaty pot pies, hot dogs, and frozen enchiladas.

The obligations food technologists have taken on for themselves have snowballed in recent years. Food has its intractable properties. Fiddle with this trait, you may have to fiddle with that one. One food technology invariably leads to another. In this way, food science has evolved into an enormous enterprise over the last decade. The output of the industry's small and large companies alike now comprises a virtual Sears and Roebuck catalogue of improved-food or food-improving characteristics.

The field of food technology is only growing. Computer analyses continue to refine our understanding of what exactly food is—stirring details for a race of people that believes now more than ever that we are what we eat. What's wrong with this picture? Well, it would appear that the average commercial farmer is going to raise his crops and livestock to suit the needs of the food processors—needs corresponding to milling machinery gauges, slaughterhouse equipment, seasonal production fluctuations, etc. So remember, if you think he isn't listening to you and your preferences, it's because you aren't his buyer anymore.

·

One of the greatest pleasures in farming, I think, is experiencing the intimate connection to food—all food, even if you personally are cultivating ten straight acres of rutabagas. Agriculture used to be closer to food—literally (geographically) as well as figuratively, and for all people. It was once, and commonly so, the province of the individual family, whose food supply was a function of its members' industriousness. In colonial times, there might have been a meadow by the home, with its small stock pasture and its fenced-in vegetable garden. You sold or traded your radishes and hams to people you knew, a system which, in small communities particularly, provided sufficient incentive for the farmer to keep his quality up and his prices equitable. The tending and farming evolved toward small-scale efficiencies and specialties—the neighbor who butchered, the fellow who owned the milking cows.

Agriculture was gradually surrendered, or bequeathed, to the concise province of fewer farmers. It's outside of our city now. It's often outside of our country. This is the geographical separation. There has similarly been a figurative separation growing between foods as we know them in the market and their simple raw agricultural counterparts in the field. Grains, meats, fruits and so on, in their elemental forms, have become more rare on the common American plate. Fewer bowls of groats, more Wonder Bread. Fewer roasts, more trays of frozen beef Stroganoff. Fewer bananas, more cans of diced fruit cocktail. This persistent polarization of raw commodity and finished food product has no doubt helped to occlude the image of the farmer, and therefore a farm consciousness, from the consumer. It continues to do so, in fact, and the gaps between farmer and consumer likewise continue to be bridged by none other than that multi-talented food processor.

The processing of farm products, as I mentioned earlier, is what differentiates raw agricultural yields from food on the plate. The separation has become so material that the U.S. government's traditional formulation of a combined food and agriculture policy has in many ways become obsolete. An easy way to comprehend the extent of this separation is by analyzing the cost of an agricultural product within the price of the final food item—for instance, the cost of the wheat used to make a one-pound loaf of bread or, put another way, the price paid to the farmer for his wheat used in that one-pound loaf. The Department of Agriculture, a bastion of numerical harvests itself, calculates what it calls the "farm value share" of a consumer's dollar. This is the portion of the dollar you spend on food which goes to the farmer. Naturally, the more highly refined or processed the food, the smaller the percentage of its price will be pocketed by the farmer. For example, USDA estimates that if you spend one dollar on a loaf of white bread, only about eight cents of that goes to the farmer for his wheat. Whereas, if in a burst of baking fever you buy one dollar's worth of wheat flour yourself, the farmer's share of your dollar will be approximately thirty-two cents. Less processing means a larger percentage of the ultimate price will go to the original farmer. If you spend one dollar on a box of eggs, the farmer will receive about two-thirds of that. Eggs don't require painstaking processing. Primarily, they need washing, sorting, and boxing. Whereas, if you buy one dollar's worth of corn flakes, the corn farmer gets six cents.

Naturally, if I were to become a corn farmer, I would only concern myself with how much I received per bushel. That's where my cost-benefit analysis would take place. I would compare the expense of land, fertilizers, seed, and so on, to the price I was receiving for my yields. A farmer can't be haunted by the potential profits yielded down the processing road by Kellogg's popping and flaking machinery in Kalamazoo, Michigan. He cannot collate his field costs with the price of a highly formulated, value-added food item.

There are definitely ways, however, by which a small farmer can capture a larger share of the consumer's food dollar. There are ways of adding value to my farm yields without necessarily expanding into the elaborate and expensive strata of food processing. First, I would say to myself, don't plant corn if you want to get rich. That just isn't the kind of crop for a small farmer to stake his pension on, much less his hopes for a bigger car. Corn is a crop that makes money in volume: "It's in the deed, American agriculture could benefit from a bright and maverick new leader to overhaul its obese, indolent, and entrenched systems (I'm referring congenially to the USDA), and to improve public perceptions, if only temporarily.

I particularly wish I had caught the segment on the radio, because the slaughter of animals for meat in this world is one of the most sticky, objectionable topics for many people to contemplate. Moreover, if you are going to raise livestock on our farm, and unless you are planning to study natural senescence in sheep, you have to confront slaughter head on. Slaughter is the bridge between animal and meat.

The British and Australians call a slaughterhouse an "abattoir," and this is indeed a relieving, euphemistic substitution of terms for those who have no knowledge of French. In the States we hear about "packing plants" and "meat packers." It is still the slaughterhouse." Livestock are "sent to slaughter." There they spend time on the "kill floor." All in all, it is not a nice language, and in off-farm company the terms connote a pretty huge bloodbath.

What I find so disconcerting about modern slaughterhouses is that live animals go in and packages of steak come out, that thousands of animals go in every day and tons of meat, and offal in various wholesale configurations come out. I believe the numbers make it bad. The numbers. The numbers of us that have resulted in the numbers of them— for burgers. We are so many, and so wealthy and so We expect meat on a daily basis, more than once a day. it cheap. We want it prepackaged and marinated if Because we are so many, we create a demand that only efficient slaughterhouses can feed. And they do feed and. They kill and skin and disembowel and butcher housands of animals each day, and that very act of e, that amplification, necessarily turns slaughterhouses not a little gruesome.

ing plants you will find the commonness of death

margins," one farmer said to me. And there are a few other crops that fall into that category—the world's staple grain crops, for example, or sugar. Instead, to increase the value of my farmland, I would head toward the more exotic items. If I intended to establish an orchard, I might try planting apple varieties that seemed to command a premium in the marketplace—Fujis, Jonagolds, Empires, or even more unfamiliar types. Some farmers I know raise curious herbs, yellow raspberries, striped peanuts, goats for milking, ducks for egg-laying, or sheep with unusual wool in order to get better prices for their goods.

The wife of a turkey farmer in Massachusetts started baking fresh turkey pot pies from their home, and within a year the demand for her pies induced her to start her own business, a complement to her husband's fresh turkey trade. I thought this was an interesting example of basic agricultural products and value-added food products being marketed side-by-side. They were earning close to a hundred percent of the farm share value for each retail turkey, and probably fifty or so percent of the farm share value on their pot pies. Their little farm operation seemed like a good argument for selling directly to the public.

"I can just see you handling the customers now," my husband said to me one day as we considered the option of a farm stand. "One funny look at your tomatoes and you'll tear them to pieces."

"Well," I said. "Why should they look funny at my tomatoes? Anyway, I'm not going to sell tomatoes. Everybody sells tomatoes."

"Eggs, then," he argued. My husband was the virtuoso on his high school debating team. "If they only want half a box, if they break one by mistake and want you to replace it, are you going to be civil?"

"Civil?" I asked.

"You're not going to bellow if they don't like our rosemary-fed lamb?" he pursued.

"I'm in the farming business," I protested, "not the food business. No farm stand. No customers."

He thought a minute.

"I know what we can call your farm," he said. "Farm from the Madding Crowd."

You could see the problem.

3

The Death Scream of the Tomato

It's a habit of mine to listen to Nati
program "All Things Considere
beans, stir onions, or devein shrimp for th
fortunately, I once missed a segment on
and only learned of it—and its graphic det
the news commentators read a number
sponding to the report. The tone of the

"Disgusting!"

"Outrageous!"

"I shall never eat pork again."

"The pig-killing was gratuitously c

"I cannot ever again feel safe lister
when my children are in the room.'

Makes you want to be a farmer,

No longer do you hear the publi
quality, cheap pork chops and ba
to curry the kind of media fav
enjoy—a little news now and ag
We hear that our cattle are des
enous vegetation. Our cropping
Our broiler operations share a

spattered all over the floors and walls, the thick and sickening smell of it, the heavy mass of spiritless flesh and wastes. Gone is the reverence man at one time felt for his stock. Gone is ritual. Gone is myth. Present are the faces of America's rural back-waters, the inbred, the poor, the transient, the illegal worker, the idiot. These are the people who kill and gut by the hour, removing the rest of us just that much farther from a basic visitation with life—and death.

The more vehement vegetarians and animal rightists would have you believe that abattoirs are second only to the World War II concentration camps in terms of genocidal brutality. If you have the opportunity to visit a slaughter plant, you will decidedly be glutted by a landscape of deep rivers of sticky hot blood, spasmodic hides and organs, butchering and the con-comitant odors of death. I don't recommend it, but then, I think there is a lot in life worth missing.

·

I was employed in the beef business when some close friends had their first baby, a boy. I went to visit with them one after-noon, and we all settled among the toy animals that littered the living room floor. We were talking about my work with cattle when Mark, the father, said, "Well, you know, we don't eat that much meat anymore." He said this into his cup of coffee.

The remark, I suppose, was meant to soften some larger un-spoken indictment of beef companies. People who have re-marked to me, "We don't eat meat," often look at me with eyes that say "You bump off guileless cows." I thought about Mark's statement. He seemed eminently relieved to have made the avowal.

"Is this a new decision?" I asked. There was a contemplative pause.

"Well," he said, "when you have a baby, it's as though you're suddenly vulnerable to all the hurt around you in this world. I know it sounds crazy, but even hurting cows—killing them and cutting them up and eating them . . . When you have a baby, you can't think about eating another animal's meat. Do you see what I mean?"

I hadn't had any children then, so I was certainly being set up to say "No," or "Maybe I'll understand when I have a baby, too." In general, I take no issue with vegetarianism, but I noticed my feathers were slightly ruffled by Mark's explanation. Many vegetarians take enormous pride in moralizing their choice, in saving savannahs worldwide, in eating a diet that is incontrovertibly closer to the gods. But here was a new angle: becoming a parent makes you an infinitely more sensitive human being, to whom red meat suddenly chills you as would violence against your own infant.

"That's interesting," I said.

Defending the slaughter of animals is not a position in which I like to find myself. I have had the chance to tour many slaughter facilities, and none is likable and I harbor an innate distrust of the employees. It is mechanized, large-scale butchering, an assembly line of disassembling, a factory whose waste is still-warm plasma and clumps of feathers. It is a form of food processing that some people argue is no different from the ripping of a plant from the soil, though I would disagree.

If you are going to raise livestock, you have to give this phase of the farming a good, hard look. My own comfort with or rationale for the modern abattoir comes from appreciating the setting of slaughter on a broad scale—how all animals treat one another in their particular "wilds." You might also find some small consolation in the fact that the killing of animals for meat has gone on for years, millennia even. Civilization has not climbed up some lonely pantophagous mountain to arrive breathless, in this brilliant twentieth century, at the villainous pinnacle of eating other earthbound animals. It's been going on, interspecies, for some time.

You might have a look at George Stubbs's eighteenth-century paintings and lithographs on the theme of the horse and the lion in the wilderness. The *White Horse Frightened by a Lion* series—even its name alone—is enough to underscore my point. The *Horse Attacked by a Lion* will drive that point home. And the *Horse Devoured by a Lion,* metaphorically or literally speaking, carries the full flavor of animal-to-animal relations. These paintings are startling to see, full of action and the idealized allegories of the animal kingdom that were in Stubbs' time the vogue. But the story is not far from an accepted truth. Animals are not what we would term chivalrous with one another in the wild. Cattle, when they have been left to fend for themselves in the wilderness, have not historically met a comfortable demise. A domestic chicken of today wouldn't survive a Boy Scout camp-out. (Its cousin, however, the wild turkey, might still give you a sense of the chicken's physically deft ancestors and their ability to survive the night alfresco.) Feral pigs are thin and fierce and perish not infrequently during their ravenous, unprovoked charges against animals much larger than themselves. Even among species beyond those we traditionally think of as livestock, there is rarely anything like "ripe old age" in the wild. Maybe that's an element in mankind's (and here I leave myself out) fixation with the Loch Ness monster. If we don't harpoon the thing, it might actually testify to its natural lifespan. Even we don't do that anymore; we outlive ours.

"My mother lives in Hilton Head and had an alligator living in the pond behind her house," said a friend of ours. "I guess the rule is that when they grow to be twelve feet, they're moved."

"Moved where?" I asked. Not here, I hoped.

"I'm not sure," she said, wrinkling her nose. "But they decided to move my mother's. They lured it out of the pond with a trail of—you won't believe this—marshmallows. A trail of tiny, fluffy white marshmallows. And sure enough, they got him.

"Actually," she added, "they finally had to shoot him because he didn't respond to about ten huge tranquilizer darts. And when they opened him up, they found a bunch of dog collars, horseshoes, and even some leather reins. It was horrible. My mother said the sheriff said these alligators drag their prey down into the water until it drowns and then they can eat it at their leisure. I said to my mother, 'Didn't you hear anything? You must have heard *something*. This alligator ate a horse right outside your bedroom window.' "

I mention this anecdote to reiterate that slaughter of livestock must be viewed in fair context. The modern abattoir can emerge as a relatively humane institution, I think, when compared to the full-scale carnage born out by one animal against another in their natural environs.

Still, the jitters of farm slaughter may not be entirely behind you. We have all grown up on grisly stories of chickens, freshly beheaded, running around the yard. Killing and butchering animals has some raw truths that take ingesting and it is also extremely strenuous—in case you were ever thinking of doing it yourself.

Assuming that slaughter isn't a task I plan to experience, raising livestock in an area remote from any public or private facility is a recipe for anguish and mayhem. I would have to hope there were individuals around who would do "that kind of thing" for me. There might be deer hunters, retired butchers, other farmers. There might even be services that haul off your animals and, a day or two later, return a nicely bagged, neatly cut-up oven-ready roast to your doorstep. Comforting. Just like the supermarket.

Some people feel, however, that one is not whole if one does not slaughter, clean, and process one's own livestock. For this sect, the USDA Cooperative Extension Service has bundles and bundles of brochures and booklets that teach the proper methodologies of slaughter. One of the publications they sent to me even highlighted the story of a young boy "dressing" (an industry word for killing, cleaning, and preparing) a mature chicken. It may be bolstering to other budding farmers to know that 4-H kids do this all the time. I found it rather intimidating.

If I were responsible for slaughtering my livestock now and

then for food, then either they or I would be senile before it happened. Guns and knives are not my forte. That's a project for the professionals at the local packing plant—if you can find them.

Twenty or thirty years ago, before cities and their suburbia consumed so much of America's rural acreage, the local packing plant was a fairly routine sight. It was often a small, unembroidered, white-washed cinderblock set back from the road. But local packing plants are hard to come by now. At the same time that developers were siting condominium clusters next to quaintly crumbling silos, the USDA started to crack down on the small slaughter operations. Upgraded sanitary and operational codes were imposed. Coolers were remodeled, pipes rerouted, walls repainted, workers retrained. Yet, in spite of all of these modernizing permutations, residents of the new condominium warrens still complained of animal sounds and smells, so many local slaughterhouses were promptly boarded up and padlocked. The ascendancy of big packing houses, such as Holly Farms or Iowa Beef Packers, with their nationwide distribution efficiency, was also a factor in the demise of the rural packing plant. These companies were just too successful at distributing cheap meat nationwide.

Wherever we establish our farm, I'll be able to locate the nearest slaughterhouse facilities by calling the State Department of Agriculture. They keep a list. I could also query my downtown butcher; sometimes these fellows custom-slaughter livestock on the side. And if we ended up in an area where deer, bear, or duck hunting is permitted, I might just ask for names from the waitress at that diner that opens at four a.m.

You might be thinking, "No thanks, I'll just stick with plant life and cropping. Harvesting a live kohlrabi is something I can do." Fair enough. Cutting roots and stems is easier to stomach than cutting jugular veins. And people generally grow less attached to individual plants over the growing season—they will more readily take scythe and tractor wheel in hand. I should add that the harvest was not always perceived in so benign a way. I've read some wonderful histories of the common tomato plant, which early botanists classified as a cousin of the deadly nightshade family. It was thought, centuries ago, that a tomato plant when pulled by its roots from the soil shrieked mercilessly in the throes of its death.

"Imagine if plants really screamed when they were harvested," said my husband. "You just couldn't live with the noise. Having a garden would be horrendous."

"In three hundred years," I said, "scientists will probably tell us that plants do scream on some heretofore inaudible frequency. What will the vegetarians say to that?"

I mused, "If it really were a high frequency, wouldn't dogs be able to hear it by now?"

"Dogs already perceive us as inhuman," my husband said.

•

"I'm not so adept at dealing with death," I said to my father one day. I was thinking about my mother, about a friend from college days now dying of AIDS, and also about my work in livestock agriculture.

"Hmmm," he said. "You're in good company. Not many people are."

"I hope I go quickly and painlessly myself," I said.

"That seems reasonable."

"Sometimes I think I would even like to die young," I added. "Miss some of the infirmities of old age. Is that cowardly?"

"Cowardly?" he considered. "I think not. Human, maybe."

Agriculture has shed new light for me on mortality. Farming's rhythm of birth and death distills the pattern of our human lives into the space of a year or two. It is an exemplar, I find, for the final meaninglessness of one's own existence—unless one acts tenaciously to make something of life either for oneself or for others. I have never felt that I had some predetermined purpose in being, other than what purpose I could construct for myself.

I am an organism, much like the others on the planet, preoccupied with mating and surviving and dying. I feel lucky not to have been a cow (although some people have told me that I already was a cow in a former life), but of course as a cow I would have been, and gratefully so, spared this cast of melancholy philosophical speculation. Listening to the news lately, I also feel fortunate not to have been born in Croatia, or Somalia, or Japan. I have enjoyed the creature comforts of being a Caucasian in America, and through the providence of that path I have been educated sufficiently to humble myself entirely.

Dust to dust. Fallow to harvest. Breeding, calving, and slaughtering. Plough under the winter rye in spring so that it may decompose and nourish the soil. I am: formed through the magnetism of molecules, the thirst of atoms for harmony, the horse-trading jumble of genetic codes, the blind pluck of the vigorous sperm. Farming brings the cycles of life home to me. Maybe that's what ultimately seems so satisfying. A small farm is not far removed from the basics of existence—the need to eat, breed and die.

"Perhaps it's because I am afraid of dying that I want a farm," I said to my father.

I was sitting in the grass while he worked in his garden—his "plantation" we affectionately called it—in Northampton. He was busy stringing twine from corner to corner, from high to low, side to side, in an eventually dense arrangement that articulated something like universal entropy. When he ran out of twine he gathered some fallen branches and poked them through the network, just so, here and there, in a pretty menacing array. This was in fact an annual ritual for him, like the autumn broadcasting of vast quantities of lime. Each spring he would create this absorbing maze—his Maginot Line, he would write in his letters—the front-line shield to protect his "crops" against the neighborhood cats.

"Well," he said, straightening his back for a moment, "that's probably more useful than creating an afterlife for yourself."

He recalibrated a branch just so.

"Tell that to Saint Peter," I brooded. "If I meet up with him at the gates, he's going to send me directly south for not believing."

My father wiped his forehead with a handkerchief. We both watched as a tiger cat wriggled through the side yard hedge and surveyed this weird architectural barrier of twine and twigs with obvious derision.

"You can tell Saint Peter you've already been there," said my father. "Farming is hell."

Part Two

Tiller

4

Le American Farmer

I will be an American farmer. American agriculture is one of the few things that still makes me proud of this country. It has not been trivialized or forsaken. It has been assaulted, slightly corrupted surely, but it nonetheless remains unparalleled throughout the world.

"Why an American farmer?" asked a friend. "Why not be a European type of farmer? That seems very painterly. The farms there are small, everything well kept—you'd feel right at home."

Sure, I thought, small farms with big subsidies and considerable instincts for self-preservation. Only a year before, my husband and I had traveled in France and observed several of their charming farmers ploughing up median strips between *les superhighways* and planting corn only French centimeters from airport runways. More recently, these enchanting agriculturalists of Europe have engaged their tractors in blocking roads instead of ploughing fields. They have been protesting the few proposals that have managed to squeak through the otherwise stymied GATT (General Agreement on Tariffs and Trade) negotiations—the Uruguay Round, which began way back when, when there were still two Germanys and one cholesterol, but which nonetheless marches on as I write, into a maturity with no graceful conclusion (just like mankind's), the continued subject of obdurate international griping and protest. This round of GATT would go down in a blaze of posturing and pettiness, I believe. *Vive le small farmer.*

"It's a question of identity," I said. "American agriculture is a piece of mine."

"I don't know. I could see you in seven aprons and a babushka."

"What do you have against American farmers?" I asked.

My friend said, "I like what they were, not what they are."

"What the American Farmer was" is a knotty national myth with deeply embedded and entangled roots. Farmer-pioneers posed at one time a plausible exemplar for the American personae (one of them, since several such personae haunt the melting pot) as the nourisher of a young nation, the valiant pathblazer, ground-tamer. How pleasing to believe that farmers are, and have always been, custodians of America's rich indigenous resources, stewards of the soil, heroes because they have made us all fat at relatively low cost.

"Not anymore," remarked my friend. "Not the big guys out West. The only thing they're custodians of is their unnumbered Swiss bank accounts full of taxpayer monies, not that I could blame them. Does the USDA help farmers set up their Swiss bank accounts?"

I said, "You think I fit the image better of a small-time Yankee farmer—"

"Maybe I'll go visit the USDA . . ."

"—spending pennies to patch my shoddy barn, steadily refining my expertise in bankruptcy law?"

She said, "Yes. That's definitely you."

A lot of our friends, when questioned, asserted that prominent differences existed among farmers and farming from one region of the country to another. Interestingly, New England farmers got a reprieve from the otherwise grievous accusations leveled against a big, impersonal agriculture "out West."

"You need a degree in chemical engineering to farm in Kansas nowadays," said one.

"I get sleepy just thinking about Nebraska," commented another.

"New England has to be more ethical about its farming," added a third. "We're packed too tightly together up here. If somebody dusts calcium arsenate over schoolyards during recess, they'll be caught."

I heard a lot of emphatic and questionably accurate refrains extolling the patrimonial virtues of Northeast farmers, sometimes generously extending down to a few Pennsylvanians. It would seem that one part of the Union possessed a lien on some ethically spotless route through agricultural history. I was surprised that so many New Englanders I spoke with distrusted the farm practices of other parts of the country, while the Yankee farming traditions remained revered. It persisted as a curious bias—the more so, I thought, considering the quick pace at which these densely populated New England states have year after year been squeezing their beloved farmers out of existence by licensing endless suburban growth. It was my own experience that while agriculture changes from one region to another, farmers by and large don't.

As an American nonfarmer of the moment, I resolved to upgrade my understanding of the American farmer, or rather the pan-American farmer. And I began my investigation at the library.

"That's a lot of books," remarked my husband observing his dinner table under siege by the various volumes. "Are you going to plant them?"

•

If you go back to the initial farmers of America, those who moored their boats off the Carolina shores in the sixteenth and seventeenth century, then they actually did have some resemblance to me. After all, they weren't farmers at all and it seems they didn't disembark from the *Tyger* prepared to cultivate their gardens. They came looking for pearls and spices, fully antici-pating that food would be sent from the larder in England or gratefully supplied by the local Indians. Not many of the first colonists survived.

"Lucky for me," I said to my husband. "Even if I fail miserably with the farm, I can still drive over to the A&P and buy groceries."

He said, "Ah, now I'm beginning to see my role in this farm more clearly: I keep my job at the bank."

I have always been drawn to the stories of the early colonists, and in particular to that of the "Lost Colony" of Roanoke, because since I was an infant my family has spent a part of its summers on the Kitty Hawk shores just a few miles away from where those first boats landed.

Kitty Hawk proper lies on the reedy peninsula of the outer banks of North Carolina, along the Atlantic coastline, south of Duck and Corolla, north of Kill Devil Hills (where, to set the record straight, the Wright brothers actually first flew) and Nag's Head. It's a very thin strip of land, a virtual sandbar, with the ocean on one side and the Albemarle and Currituck Sounds on the other. From many points along the dune crests you can overlook both bodies of water at once.

There were few houses at all here in the 1960s, and most of those looked remarkably alike—cinderblock matchboxes painted in garish pastels, every window shaded with a bleached-out canvas awning. The driveways were sand and the main road, too, turned to sand just yards from our house. In the first years of our southerly pilgrimage, my mother would go to retrieve buckets of fresh water from a pump at the end of the concrete road. The local telephone was miles away at the edge of "town," in a booth in front of Anderson's Trading Post. At Anderson's was the gasoline pump, stamps, and last week's newspapers with a growl from Mrs. A. The grocery store, Winks, was eight miles away, and it, too, was a tiny pink cinderblock building with big awnings out front.

As a child, I was always surprised that the colonists had had the wits to sail beyond this sandy beach into the Pamlico and Albemarle Sounds. How did they know to go further? Well, and it was a good thing they did, I decided then, because past the hot sand dunes and their rippling densities of golden sea oats—in no way predisposed to farming—was a serene and fertile mainland, with cornfields, jam stands, and watermelon patches.

Each summer my sisters and I would plead with our parents to see *The Lost Colony,* an evening outdoor theater production in Manteo, across the sound from Nag's Head. My mother usually surrendered herself to the chore, year after year able to recite more of the play by heart. As she drove us across the bridge onto the mainland, I remember the earth suddenly changing into pine forest and peach groves, cucumber patches and soybean fields. From the back seat of our station wagon, I would gaze out, speculating that this area had offered the first colonists the best of both worlds—a beach for floating in their inner tubes, and right across the waterway, a farm where they could buy fresh tomatoes, just like we did. Each year this trip to see *The Lost Colony* seemed equally magical and mysterious, and I felt *anybody* would get lost in that pine forest at night, the small paved road almost lost to shifting sands and pine needles, and with no street lights to boot.

We slapped mosquitoes as Sir Walter Raleigh authorized the building of the first fort, and we turned our attention from the night sky's shooting stars when Agona, the comic Indian squaw, finally arrived on the stage fat and moaning and scouting out a suitable brave—lips pursed and rouged, eyes wide, corn husks shshshing from her primitive clothing and feathers drooping from her hair.

"Not a particularly attractive rendering of the Indians," sighed my mother as we drove home afterward. And indeed, there had been a lot of angry ones, whooping war cries and torching the British settlements. In recreating a moment in history about which there is scarcely any information available, this play had proffered a distinctly biased point of view.

"Maybe you should call your farm The Lost Colony," my husband suggested, "as a kind of memorial for those early farmers and settlers."

"That doesn't seem very propitious," I said. "Besides, I'd probably be sued for attempting to arouse anti-Indian sentiment."

"Mmmmm," he ruminated. "How about calling it A Maizing Grace."

The American farm did ultimately grow into a preserve of the rumored abundance. Forests were pushed back and kept at bay. Breeding stock was imported. Ploughs were refined. Corn and tobacco were exported. Corn and tobacco are still exported, and in profusion.

Tobacco, for all of its ills, always struck me as a kind of celebrity commodity within a peculiarly American heritage. The fields covered with cream-colored gauze netting and the slatted drying barns must be homey images for anyone raised in western Massachusetts—even those who don't smoke.

My grandfather worked as a young boy in a cigarette factory in the Bronx. The factory was housed in a five-storey building, and there were large holes cut in the floors from one storey down to another. The finest cigarettes, he said, were manufactured with the best tobacco on the top floor. The stray leaf shavings that fell in the normal course of business were periodically swept through the holes in the floor and rained into the leaf bins of the storey below, where lesser grade cigarettes were rolled. From floor to floor the sweepings fell and the quality slipped, and on the ground floor workers were allowed to grab handfuls of the cheapest cigarettes to take home each evening.

It's a marvelous image. When I think about tobacco today, however, it is in connection either with smoking, which is a filthy habit no matter how charming cigarette assembly ever was, or with lung cancer, which has played a fatal role in America's ugly litigious streak. So I called up the Department of Agriculture to find out what was doing with tobacco as a crop these days.

"Tobacco is the sixth-largest cash crop in America," beamed a USDA expert (between puffs, I imagined) on the end of the line. "We're still the world's major exporter."

"Terrific," I said.

"Well, of course, tobacco production is supported by the government," he said.

"I see," I said. "You mean we subsidize tobacco production, and then our Secretary of Health says 'Don't smoke, it'll kill you,' and then people die from lung cancer and we pay their lawyers to lose battles with the big cigarette companies."

(Puff, puff)

Me: "That's the American way, I guess."

He sent me a pamphlet full of charts and numbers and projections. It had a glossary in the back which gave me a richer impression of tobacco farming, in the same way that studying any language gives you a better sense of a culture (German being adjective-impoverished, for example). As I glanced through the glossary of terms, I developed a more elaborate image of tobacco's agriculture—the three dominant varieties of snuff, the "tipping" of the leaf to remove unwanted stem. "Prizing," I learned, refers to the packing of tobacco into "hogsheads," large, round wooden casks that store about one thousand pounds each of tobacco leaf for aging. Many of the terms retained a kind of colonial resonance to them, as though high technology had somehow bypassed the tobacco leaf; but interspersed, of course, were telling modern expressions like No-Net-Cost Act of 1982 or Price Supports.

Several elements of America's tobacco story echo elements of our broader agricultural background. Tobacco was a modest crop, for instance, before the colonists found a variety, the Orinoco, that was greatly preferred in the European markets. Suddenly every colonial farmer wanted to share in the windfall. That's a healthy capitalist urge. Exports exploded. Ships sagged. In 1616, so many farmers were planting tobacco that the governor of Virginia had to order the planting of at least two acres of corn to ensure adequate food stocks for the domestic population. It's not de facto that Americans always dash to extremes (although I wouldn't deny it), but perhaps that we have historically been an industrious, entrepreneurial lot.

Supply and demand. Subjugation of natural resources. Wringing profits from an often begrudging wilderness. This is the tradition, I have mused to myself in quiet moments of doubt, that I will perpetuate. These are the footsteps of exploitation that I will advance.

But of course there is a wonderfully ingenious and inventive side of that tradition, too. There were individuals for whom commercial instinct was tempered by loftier sensitivities. There have been farmers with ambitions to improve the national agriculture, to invent better farming equipment, or to ameliorate the agrarian situation. Thomas Jefferson is an easy example to cite. He researched and promoted better sheep breeds, he experimented with new crop strains, he designed more effective tools—then he wrote it all down. He kept meticulous records of his daily farm chores, harvests, weather, costs, and concepts. It can't be overly stressed that such journals were key in developing American agriculture. It flourished as much by dint of clever observation as it did by dint of physical domination.

"I guess this is where you and farming part ways," said my husband. "You're not big on recordkeeping." He looked up at me as if to punctuate the gravity of this character-based obstacle.

"I have a very intuitive side," I said, jocular, trying to avert a discussion. I can't stand these self-reforming discussions. I come from a family in which improving oneself was a pastime.

"Keeping up a good journal is critical," he pursued, "if you're going to take this farm seriously."

Did he say "seriously"? Outrage. I stifled a caustic observation.

This interchange warrants a brief digression from the subject of farm journals, I think. I have always tried to look benignly upon constructive criticism, and it might be said that I ordinarily fail. That is, I hear and mostly accede to reproof, but I don't always do it with a smile. If I obliged myself a defense, it would be that constructive criticism does tend to arrive at the most inopportune moments in life, when one, in the height of a lost humor, has done something correspondingly inferior and thus invited somebody's (a witness's) enlightening suggestions for rehabilitation. Thank you, I would like to say. Thank you for caring so much about me as to concern yourself with the fine-tuning of my dedicatedly narrow-minded wrongdoings.

Aaahh. What a good farmer I shall make, immune to all propositions of change.

I say that with humor, since farmers are not so immutable as nonfarmers like to believe, and since for a budding farmer constructive criticism is indeed not only invaluable but desired. When I become a farmer, I will be a maladroit beginner again, soliciting tips whenever possible from the already entrenched. Criticism in such instances is not denunciation, but guiding analysis. It took farming for me to want to be a beginner again, to want to start all over, like a child. I am grateful for that liberty since it is self-renewing. Do we all have a place, I wonder, where the old defenses dry up and drop off and where one feels the glorious side of Vulnerable?

Having said that, I can admit my husband was perfectly right that I am no natural recordkeeper. I might even let him know it, though his criticism in no way came on the wings of loving intonation. Mmm-hmm, he will certainly be surprised to see the zest with which I maintain a farm journal. One cannot know where Possibility lies in another.

To probe and to prepare, I took a copy of Jefferson's farm journal from the library one afternoon to see how he had arranged it.

"March 28, 1771: planted 5. grapes from N. Lewis's on S.E. edge of garden."

"March 24, 1803: a considerable snow on the blue ridge."

"May 28, 1811: artichokes come to table. The last dish is July 28."

"I'm going to need a lot of pencils," I smiled to my husband. "Just so that I don't miss a thought, you know, between feed bunk and stall for instance."

"We could set up a laptop computer in the barnyard," he said. "And everytime you walked by you could type in your notes: chicks still fairly cute this morning; tell Chuck to feed animals before going to bank; went to Stop & Shop to check out lettuces of competitors—depressing—came home and talked to goat."

•

I met a man who said he had introduced turkeys to Switzerland, or rather, had introduced the Swiss to turkeys. Well, and before that he had spent a couple of years on a sheep farm in New Zealand, and after that he had spent a year on a pig farm in southern England. He had even worked on dairy farms in Switzerland before getting a degree and moving into the food business. There wasn't much about farm management that would surprise him, he said. One day he told me about pigs from Mongolia with four inches of coarse, unmarketable hair, and when I said I had never heard of such a thing he said, "And you say you're in agriculture?"

His name was Martin and he was a Swiss man with a penchant for untangling the manure problems of farmers in the Alps. But when he was finished with that, well, he didn't know what. Maybe he would help the American farmers solve their problems.

"I am quite through with turkeys," he said. "Now everybody knows. They know a turkey."

I told Martin about my farming intentions.

"Maybe I could raise those longhaired Mongolian hogs," I smiled.

I was genuinely interested in less run-of-the-mill breeds of stock, even if that meant pigs. Secondary breeds—cattle deemed too small, sheep that mature too slowly, chickens whose breasts are not enormous—several minor breeds have been pushed toward extinction by modern agriculture's pragmatic inclinations to streamline and standardize. Threatened farm animal breeds have suffered the added disadvantage of being overlooked by most animal protection groups. I'm not sure why. There are resolute environmentalists who will lie down on train tracks for a Dutch salamander but who think of rare livestock breeds as an altogether other sphere. I remarked to Martin about my specific interest in minor breeds and I asked him to let me know when he came across other unusual illustrations.

"It is good," said Martin, "to raise the older breeds on your farm. It is good, this idea for a small operation. You just keep ten percent of your animals in the barn and ninety percent in the freezer."

"In the freezer?" I asked. I knew what he was aiming at, but his delivery made me incredulous.

"Yah, naturally," he said. "You must breed your animals, take their embryos, put them in the freezer. Everyone in America does it, I think. You need one barn, one freezer. It is very efficient. One barn, one freezer."

Embryo transfer is an interesting if not wholly reliable practice. It is still considered by some to be one of biotechnology's many infants, with all the flaws and doubts and questions accorded as a rule to infants—with the exception of human babies, who, if you ask their mothers, are indeed flawless. Embryo transfer is, however, a quick and effective way of introducing animals to foreign environments. A cattle embryo with considerable genetic value can be transplanted into a recipient cow in Burundi, say, and the calf during gestation will take on the diverse disease immunities of its local mother. A Mongolian long-haired pig embryo implanted in an agreeable pink York-shire sow . . . And embryos frozen in liquid nitrogen are infinitely more portable than a herd of livestock. It's logistically advantageous. One sleeps easier not having to figure out how to supervise a 747 jumbo jet packed with nervous pregnant heifers, quarantine here quarantine there, then onto the trucks without the springs and over the roads without the pavement to some rural bovine research facility deprived of electricity as we know it and certain supplies of hay as we like it, and crowing with new bugs—the ones you do see and the ones you don't.

"Good concept," I said to Martin. "Embryos are quieter, too."

"Yah," he said with a face that showed he didn't get my joke. It's hard to get jokes in other languages. There's been some controversy, too, about the genius of my jokes in general.

I said, "I'll have to find myself a willing veterinarian with liquid nitrogen on tap."

"Yah," Martin agreed. "In fact you should have your freezer there. It is more efficient."

He added, "You don't need a big American freezer, you know. A smaller model—I show you—is energy-efficienter."

"I would worry about electricity however," I mused. "One shortage, one circuit overload, and I'll have killed hundreds of seven-celled cows and goats."

"Yes, alzo," said Martin, never at a loss for solutions, "you need to keep things separated. For safety. In case the electricity breaks or so. You should have your freezer somewhere else. Or two freezers is maybe best. Two barns, two freezers."

Two barns, two freezers. Two refrigerators for all the pharmaceutical paraphernalia. Two ovens to boil the water to sterilize the instruments. Two vets to ready the cows to synchronize heats to accept the embryos . . . This was not what I had had in mind.

"Just think," said Martin. "The bigger your freezers, the

smaller your farm has to be. Land is expensive. It is a very efficient way to carry on."

•

Mongolian pigs with four inches of coarse hair are probably not in the cards for me. Pigs, overall, are not my favorite barnyard residents, although I have always enjoyed visiting other people's pigs. When I was a student of agricultural economics at Texas A&M, I used to visit the university farm centers in my free time and watch the students perform their research or husbandry chores.

At A&M, the world of agriculture is neatly aggregated across acres and acres of rolling farmland. There are cotton fields that seem to bloom snow in the autumn. There are peanut fields that yield maroon-and-white (the Texas Aggie colors) striped peanuts for insatiable alumni. There are sorghum fields where scientists make incursions into the problems of lodging (toppling over) stalks. There are poultry houses and a dairy where, I'm told, the real live Borden Milk's Bessie, a Jersey cow, plods out her productive days in between show appearances. One of my favorite excursions was to the Swine Center, where I could walk through the farrowing barn and see the sows flouncing around beside their umpteen blind and squirming piglets. They certainly weren't worried about any final exams.

Usually a group of students would be chatting in the anteroom of the little administrative building. They all wore coveralls and Texas Aggie baseball caps. (Soon, I thought, they would be wearing smart new caps sporting the logos of various swine pharmaceutical firms.) This small office was crowded with metal desks and filing cabinets, the ubiquitous coffeemaker, a water cooler, and a coat rack with white lab coats and plastic boots for visitors with shoes worth saving. The walls were adorned with humorous pig posters and Texas Aggie sports calendars. The students came to recognize me after a while, and would wave me on through the door to the barns. They enjoyed their work and swine research, but they thought it was hilarious that I would come to the center—and more than once—just to look around.

"Where you from anyway?" they would ask, their young, earnest faces tipped up under their caps. Altogether, they were a most good-natured and bright group of people. They became part of my pleasure in visiting the Swine Center. I found that after weeks of studying U.S. farm policy and its corpulent, inbred bureaucratic programs, I was invariably refreshed to see these students, with their enthusiasm and spirited outlook, learning the ropes of farm management. The same could be said for the rosy-cheeked group that worked out at the Dairy Center. This was the next generation of American farmers, and it was heartening.

Beyond the students' office was a hallway that led to the pens.

"They still look the same," a voice would call after me, laughing.

And then another, "Give the girls my regards."

Then came a helpful remark, "Pen thirteen farrowed last night."

Once I shouted back, "Oh my gosh, what happened? Where are all the animals?" It produced the desired stampede. "Just kidding," I smiled, as four panting bodies spilled into the barn behind me. So, truce, laughter, the end of traded quips. I was offered a coffee and I drank it as though puffing on a peace pipe.

Before walking through the long farrowing barns, visitors were required to step in a plastic pail of iodine, a "dip." It sat by the doorway, looking as innocent as turtle soup while it ruined one pair of unsuspecting shoes after another. Straight ahead lay long lines of farrowing pens separated by cement walkways. Cement, for all of its plain ugliness, has become extremely useful to farmers. It is easy to hose clean, easy to drive vehicles over, and terrific for anchoring iron posts. The larger the farm, the more critical seem its advantages.

Each small farrowing pen was divided in two with a piece of widely slatted iron fencing. In one half lay the sow—enormous—on her side, with her front hooves splayed forward in front of her snout and her rear legs stretched taut and vertically downward, like a ballet dancer's, toes ever so lightly grazing the pen wall. Less graceful were the occasional grunts, the snout that, even in slumber, seemed to be rooting through the straw-covered flooring for a stray turnip or truffle. This was Mom, to a litter not infrequently of over twelve little piglets that were sequestered for their own protection on the other half of the pen. They could reach readily through the iron slats for one of her many paired teats, but she could not roll over onto them in her soundest sleep and unwittingly suffocate the lot—as sows are known to do handily. So it is not uncommon on pig farms to find divided farrowing pens. On the one side lies the sow with her teats exposed; on the other side a pink brawl of siblings, blind at birth and relying on their wonderful noses to detect a promising source of milk.

Baby pigs, piglets, are unusually adorable. They call out to one's most rudimentary instincts to be held and murmured to. Warm, nuzzling, smooth, soft and uttering improbably endearing noises. Mankind would become an absolute slave to piglets if only they didn't grow into pigs (thus are we saved). I heartily recommend a visit to a pig farm for anyone not yet exposed to the scene of fourteen two-day-old piglet siblings fast asleep on top of one another, settled into a sweet pink heap of communal breathing that can only be likened to a napping rugby scrum. However, cast your glance then a little to the left and you will likely be introduced to their gargantuan mother, perhaps six hundred pounds of her, in a less endearing hide—a sight which, though a rude shock, may be considered sensibly bracing. It's a question of temperament.

I'm not drawn to hogs, although some of the smaller breeds have caught my attention lately. I have heard that they are surprisingly bright, like to stay clean, and make great pets. The more exotic breeds are growing fastest in popularity. There is a flourishing pet market in the States, for example, for the Vietnamese potbellied pig, a very small, very round pig that has captured the hearts of many wealthy pet lovers apparently bored with the usual cat-and-dog fare.

"We were going to get one of those Vietnamese pigs," said a neighbor of ours in Greenwich. "But we went over to some friends' house—they have one—and honestly, there was the pig, this fat, round thing, sitting on the couch with their kids, watching TV and eating grapes. And when the thing got bigger, you could barely see its eyes for the big folds of fat that hung down over them. You'd have to have these . . . these eyebrow flabs surgically held up or I don't know—the thing would be blind. All I can say is that the thing loved peanut butter."

The thing. That was certainly not a hard sell for anyone window-shopping the pet pig markets. I follow neither the pet pig markets nor the commercial hog markets. The image of pork belly futures trading or frozen pork bellies traveling cross-country on our railroads seizes my sense of comic whimsy, but the business itself holds no allure. Apart from pickled pig's knuckles, which I rightly or wrongly associate with Jewish holidays, pigs and pork are for me a thing of Chicago and the Midwest. And not a sanguine thing. I come across swine-industry articles in my stock magazines that shed some light for me on the modernization of the pig industry. It seems that pigs lend themselves to certain industrialized efficiencies and needs that mean fewer farmers, more cages and microchips. It sounds not unlike the poultry industry.

On the efficiency side, I have heard of farmers stacking pigs in slightly tipped battery cages—similar to what is now done with laying hens. The pigs are kept thus raised and confined for their few months before slaughter, and the handling of the cages is easier for farmers than the handling of live loose pigs. Such confinement systems are always designed to give a farmer more control over the animals and their environment, and to reduce his demand for labor. One farmer can husband hundreds of pigs by himself, but I would add that it is rarely referred to as animal husbandry at that point—rather, it is farm industry management.

On the matter of needs, pigs are relatively demanding. They require strict temperature controls. They cannot survive lengthy periods of strong heat, for instance. Pigs do not sweat and this is why you often see them immobilizing themselves in mud puddles or sinking like a plug into their own water troughs during the hot summer months. And pigs have similar luck with extended months of cold.

"In the wintertime," said one hog farmer, "I use hot-air blowers in the barns, but even that's not enough. I put down a bed of straw that's about thigh-high—no funniness here—and the pigs just burrow in there to get warm and you might as well think you didn't have any pigs around at all. You might be raising a barn of two hundred hogs but when you look inside, all you see is straw. You got to wait till spring if you want any ham. Fortunately, o'course, that's about when Easter happens."

I was told that another meaningful aspect of the pig industry is that it is essentially a traffic in minors.

"Market hogs are all very young," explained a veterinarian to me. "They're usually a matter of months old when they're shipped off. And so they are extremely susceptible to child contagions."

Child contagions, I thought. It had the ring of child labor. I asked if this were the reason for the iodine tubs at Texas A&M's Swine Center.

"It was not so much for you and your shoes," the vet said, "but for visiting hog farmers who may be carrying on their shoes the parasites or bacteria from farms with pigs not immunized or not genetically secure from these infant diseases."

I have watched market hogs, their snouts constantly sweeping along the grubby ground of their pens in search of some savory curiosity or overlooked scrap of lettuce. It was clear they were putting themselves in harm's way. But *children,* I kept thinking. I couldn't rinse the image from my head.

I would add, lastly, that pigs have proven problematic on the farmer-friendly concrete floors that garnish so many modern-day stock barns. Because of the anatomical inflexibility of their little hocks, their bodies take a beating on the hard surface and they develop what is called porcine stress syndrome, or PSS. PSS can lead to various degrees of injury. I have heard of prize boars sold at auction who are discovered later to be useless because they cannot mount a female—poor back legs. I have heard of paralysis and malaise. Moreover, pigs suffering from PSS often yield inferior meat with visibly detracting properties. PSE stands for pale soft exudate and it refers in no euphemistic way to the runny fat that can characterize the meat of pigs afflicted with PSS. It looks rank.

Instead of surrendering the convenience of concrete, many pig farmers buy floor-surface coverings of slatted or punctured plastic, equally easy to clean and sanitize but billed as more sympathetic to the hoof and hock. This is the way of all farming, I think—the growth of technologies that, whether in the right direction or the wrong, escalate and become mutually dependent. They turn a farmer from husbandman to businessman and they focus his concerns on questions like: In stacking my battery cages four instead of three high, what is the marginal profit? Do I need to switch industrial cleaning agents when I use green plastic flooring instead of plain concrete? The cleaning agent specially designed to clean this green flooring has an overpowering hygienic scent; do I need to improve my ventilation system to ensure my pigs stay healthy after I clean? This farmer is taking logical, maybe profitable steps. They develop, however, into a type-A bureaucratic snowball.

This technology-avaricious behavior is not exclusive to the swine industry. Consider the case of a poultry farmer. It used to be he sold Grade AA large white eggs in the local markets as fast as he and his wife could collect them and box them. In

1982, however, cash-register receipts analyzed by the grocery store's Profit-Center-Management-Information system (a computer) were indicating that he had to switch to a flock of brown-egg layers to keep his consumers satisfied, although it is widely known that there is no difference between white and brown eggs apart from color. So he found a "cross" (a hybrid hen) in Ohio that suited his needs, and replaced his entire flock—old hens to the soup pots, new pullets (female chicks) to the roost. Then egg consumption dropped off because of cholesterol worries, and he had to switch breeds again, this time to some layer cross shipped out of Missouri with a name that looked like a license plate—but a hen from whom he could get at least two dozen more eggs per year than out of the former breed, which meant he could cut his total flock by maybe twenty percent. He condensed barns, lay concrete for a shipping dock, installed conveyor belts and dust control systems along the walls. When times kept getting tougher in the egg business, he found that by substituting battery cages four high in lieu of his floor system (this meant moving the whole dust control system, which is a critical component of poultry operations, to ceiling connections), he could let go his last hired hand and manage the whole operation—electrical gadgetry willing—by himself with help from his wife.

What will become of my small farm? And me without a wife.

5

Ploughshares and Microchips

A ranch hand I once worked with told me, between spits of chewing tobacco juice, that I looked grrrreat on a tractor. What I replied doesn't bear the vituperative spelling out. What I felt was fury. I had faced sexual innuendo before, in office jobs, in school, on public transportation—most women do—but to find it on this ranch, in the midst of my workday, while I was in layers of filthy blue jeans and sweatshirts and struggling to put an old John Deere 435 into third gear, completely galled me. It made me venomous.

My anger came not so much from an assault on my feminist self. I am, as my mother once said of herself, a "flawed feminist." My anger came from the unsolicited intrusion of a profound, corrosive element to my state of mind *à la ferme*. Don't you ruin my agriculture, I was smoldering with your trite, invasive remarks.

I had found such a welcome respite from sexual concerns in ranch work, a peace in the manual labor, the pulling of irrigation lines, the rewinching of barbed wire fences, or the hauling of kitchen orts out to the pigs. I was certainly not as strong or mechanically adept as the other hands who were male, but I had my own chores and I could manage them alone. After this comment, it was hard for me to get up onto the rusting old John Deere without feeling self-conscious. Had I tucked in my several layers of shirts? Should I have? What was playing into his hands and what wasn't? I resented this burden, and I found it especially nettlesome since driving old tractors is rarely either comfortable or easy. On that 435, for instance, one had to wear earphones to cope with the roar and rattle. The exhaust pipe, with its cap flapping over the furrows, sent diesel fumes like champagne spume to the nose, throat, and eyes. The springs, as capable as ornament, tossed one's body up and down and left and right across the hard, molded leather seat. I used to have to hang onto the steering wheel to keep from being hurled off. How, I wondered, could that be a prrrretty sight?

I remembered this incident as I was trying to think back to what exactly the ranch had used its crumbling collection of tractors for—I was wondering whether I would need a tractor on my own small farm. Well, we had used them to pull the aluminum irrigation pipes from one alfalfa bay to the next. We had used them to haul the manure-spreader out onto the cultivated fields. And we had used them to pull other ranch vehicles (including the other tractors) out of the mud or snow. I polled my husband.

"Do you need a tractor," he contemplated. "That's a good question because, as you say, it's a function of what they're needed to pull or push. If you're not cultivating crop land, I guess you can get by without. You certainly don't need one for a garden." And here the eyebrows fluttered up and down suggestively. "But it would be great fun."

My husband is not as machine-averse as I. Tractors. All I could imagine was their noise.

"Maybe we could borrow or rent one," said my husband, "at the beginning, to help set fence posts and things like that."

This seemed sensible. Depending on how small a farm is, tractors may not be crucial for day-to-day operations. I could traffic square bales here and there in the bed of a pick-up truck—and since I already owned a small one, I felt, smugly, entirely ready to start buying livestock. I also had in the back of my mind the advice of several farmers. Above all, they have cautioned me, the biggest mistake new farmers make is to run out and buy everything first. Most of them agreed, too, that buying new equipment was almost always money down the drain. There's always a good used tractor, a good used plough-share, a good used hay wagon to be found. One farmer I knew in Danbury made this point and then pulled a long white sheet of paper from the glove compartment of his truck. It was the *Connecticut Agricultural Marketing Newsletter,* and it contained three long columns, thinly fretted with advertisements for land, machinery, animals, and help. It was farmers talking to farmers. Tractors, combines, electric fencing, silage choppers, whole farms, Toggenburg goats—the future seemed to be availing itself to me, weekly, and for extremely moderate prices. I subscribed.

The issue of tractors is a simple and economic one. Either the farm is so small you don't depend on one, or the farm is— grows—large enough that you need the help. Labor is expensive. We'll do what we can by ourselves and when ourselves are inadequate we'll look to machinery to assist us before we look toward hiring employees. The tractor purchase would wait. It was with this patient, head-screwed-on-right feeling that I would occasionally browse through farm equipment dealerships to see how tractors were evolving and to get a better sense of what horsepower—that wholly mysterious and ironic word—meant.

"I don't mean to butt in, hon," a Kubota tractor dealer in New York said to me, "but I think you're making a mistake. In all honesty, I think you've got things backward."

I had been perambulating his outdoor exhibit of small trac-tors, an acre or more of husky orange just-over-lawn-mower-size models set up so that you had to slalom in and out between thorny cultivating and planting attachments. I had told him no, I wasn't needing anything yet. My farm wasn't even established.

"In my mind," he went on, "a tractor is about the very first thing you *do* want to buy, and a solid one, too. Tractors aren't just a way of hauling hay, you know."

"You're probably right," I said, not because I thought he was but because this usually quiets salesmen. He was immune.

"Ask me your questions," he pushed. Obviously the Japanese were now schooling their American sales forces to get cozy with customers. "Tell me what's holding you back."

The Psychiatric Approach to Tractor Selling, by Yuki-san Moto Kubota.

"Well," I said, scanning for a question that might be hanging around the right side of my brain. "What I would really like to know is why tractor dealers and farmers keep their equipment outside in all weather? Aren't you people worried about rust?"

"Rust? Why our Kubotas are practically invincible. You're looking at layers and layers of paint on every part of the body. Layers and layers."

"You would want me to keep this in a barn or garage, wouldn't you?" I asked.

"Well," he said, "yes, naturally."

"Hmmmm," I ruminated. Question dodged. I was getting a little edgy, feeling engulfed in a profusion of identical pygmy tractors. It was like a lawn full of matchbox cars—for Goliath. Every tractor was bright and gaily colored, the wheels jet black with rubber polish—all a little big for under the Christmas tree, but panting to be played with. I imagined an *Alice in Wonderland* tag on a steering wheel: START ME.

Most other people circulating through the outdoor showcase seemed to be there for the sunny-day fun of it, or because "he" just can't stop buying machines. "It's a disease," I heard one wife say, beaming happily in the shadow of such buying power. I couldn't spot anyone there that looked like a farmer. Everyone was neatly dressed in polo shirts and khakis, the uniform for Sunday shoppers in upper Westchester County.

"When the time is right, I think I will be hunting up something a little larger," I finally said to the salesman, who had been dogging me, his hands constantly smoothing his hair. He was not going to give me up for anything. These other shoppers, well, they were there to buy. They could wait. But me, I was going to be trouble.

So I reiterated, "In any case, I'm not going to buy anything today. I'm just here to see the alternatives and the attachments."

"Honey," he said, "I can tell you right now that these little babies are twice as powerful as any midsize Case or John Deere you're ever like to find. We have got performance figures that completely blow them out of the water. These Kubotas are bona fide nuggets of power."

The "bona fide" caught my attention. I love to hear the unexpected words that turn up in various vocabularies.

I said, "Hmmmm."

He said, "You wait right here a minute, hon, and I'll run inside and get you some of our brochures. You'll be able to read the figures for yourself. Or," he paused with something akin to a leer, "would you like to test drive one of these girls?" He waved his arm in a broad arc across his amber field of engine blocks and wheel shields. He thought he had me now. "Hon" on one of the "girls."

"No," I said. "I appreciate the offer. To tell you the truth, I'm pretty confident I want an American tractor." I smiled. "We all draw lines in funny places, don't we, fella?"

•

Thomas Jefferson was, among other things, a serious student of plough design, and he had tried to budge American farmers of his time from their complacency with ineffectual implements. The early ploughs had been made of wood and often owned not by the farmer but by an independent ploughman. This ploughman would bring his plough and oxen over to your farm under contract, but since all farmers in a region do their sowing and harvesting around the same time, they must have vied strenuously to get his assistance before seed rotted, rains came, or harvests spoiled. I told my husband about this snag. He loves these sorts of stories.

"That probably marks the birth of extortion in America," he said merrily. "And what a big day that was."

The day of the independent ploughman was short-lived, with obvious reason. By the time Jefferson came along, the farmer owned his own plough, useless as it might be. I usually close my eyes when I see mechanical drawings, graphs, charts, and the like on a page, but I became interested in Jefferson's plough sketches because they were so simple and graceful, and they provided me with an elemental grasp of the concepts behind farm machinery, which I otherwise would have tried to ignore. The high-technology engines that combust down modern-day farm rows completely cow me, and I suspect I could not hope ever to grasp the theories behind their formulation. If you look at early farm implements, however, you can begin to comprehend the purposes and problems of their design. You can grapple at least in theory with the basic ideas of strength, durability, precision, and handling. From there, I infer, even if you add a few fuses, catalytic converters, hydraulic adjusters, digital analogs, and air conditioning, you can still recognize in today's high-tech tractors and combines some antiquated threads of basic engineering objectives that have steered the course of modernization since the earliest unavailing apparatus.

Among the first ploughs used to turn up American soil were the "bull ploughs." It took two men—one behind the plough, one leading the oxen—and often four to eight oxen to prepare a field. These early ploughs cut perhaps three inches into the soil, and the arduous process, accented by frequent pauses for repairs, resulted in an average of only one acre ploughed per day. One acre. Well, and any gardener can tell you three inches is not very deep when it comes to cultivating the ground. My husband and I faced this problem when we first set up a vegetable garden in our Connecticut backyard.

"We recommend you turn over a foot if you can," said our local nurseryman. "You got a rototiller?"

"No," I replied.

"Yah, well, can you get one?"

The point was being made.

"Let's suppose I couldn't," I said. "How deep now?"

"Is it sod?" he asked.

"Yes."

"For how long?"

"I don't know."

"You don't know?" There was silence. "You know, sometimes it gets kind of compacted. We recommend you get it rototilled."

"I've got a fork," I said. "About how deep?"

"About a foot."

We did eventually get the plot turned over by hand, and later our neighbors expanded it substantially with their stout little tractor and its rototiller attachment. We compared the small garden we had prepared ourselves to the larger plot of tractor-tilled land. The hand work had been far less successful in terms of aerating and breaking up the clay clods in the soil, and it had brought home all the more the difficulties of clearing new land. We, at least, had had the advantage of steel forks and shovels. The early farmers effectively had only wood.

Our interest piqued, we drove over to a farm museum in Stamford to see some such wooden tools. We walked by walls of ash, hickory, and chestnut pitchforks that showed the meticulous craftsmanship of colonial woodworkers, who sought to provide the least resistance and the most strength to the wielder. These forks were beautiful and fluid, but they seemed incredibly fragile and sometimes cumbersome for their long handles. The young woman at the museum explained that the longer handles were used to gain leverage on rocks and roots.

"They bent," she said. "They were very useful."

We were skeptical.

Iron, like a godsend, became more accepted among agricultural implements after the Revolutionary War. Ironic, I think, the way war historically seems to spawn a kind of inventiveness that assumes a benign form for gutted populations in its aftermath. Farmers would take their wooden tools over to the local blacksmith, who would attach pieces of iron sheeting, for reinforcement, to the ground-cutting surfaces. I relate more to the farmers who, I learned, desperately nailed old horseshoes, scrap-iron bits, and used hoe blades onto their ploughshares—anything available to fortify the edge and slow the wear and tear. Plain wood shares against a dense grass or clay or compacted soil were nearly futile—not unlike those little plastic knives the deli will give you to do combat against their steak sandwiches.

The plough predicament was critical, and it was exacerbated by widespread sentiment among farmers that cast iron infected the soil and fostered weeds. With perceptions such as these, it's not surprising that American farmers missed the agricultural revolution that occurred in England in the eighteenth century. But they were not too far behind. In 1837, an Illinois blacksmith by the name of John Deere picked up the used blade of a worn-out mill saw. It was made of tough Sheffield steel. Deere engineered this blade into a functional plough that was able to make quick work of the thick and claylike prairie soils. Under this plough, American farmland blossomed.

As a prospective American farmer myself, I hope I might operate with less resistance to change than some of these early farmers—but then, as a small farmer, I suspect there will be little high-technology instrumentation beating a path to my barn door.

·

When it comes to farm equipment and machinery, there are definitely ways to stay ahead of the pack. Computers offer a multiplicity of labor-substituting or labor-facilitating options suitable for many of the short-distance, regular-interval chores that take place inside a barn. The daily cadence of these chores lends itself to computerized *systems,* and we are truly a culture spellbound by systems and systems management.

I adore systems, probably more than the next guy. I loll in the familiarity of routine. When my day is ordered, it assuages my sense of internal chaos and I sometimes think I would be the last to grumble if all days were thoroughly alike. This is anathema to my husband, who flourishes within the tactical confines of computer systems, but for whom eating chicken twice in one week is a surrender to life's encroaching monotony. He will be the one to put lighting timers in the barn, and he will be the one to take DOS by the horns and fashion some wonderful farm-budget and livestock-performance programs for me on the computer.

"Think of the Lotus spreadsheets we can make," he said enthusiastically one evening. "Column after column after column on your sheep."

"I'm actually better with paragraphs than columns."

"You'll get the hang of this in no time," he continued. "And once you've got everything in Lotus, I've got a program that turns it into terrific charts and graphs. It's incredible."

"I can't read bar charts," I mumbled. "Did I ever tell you that? Besides, who's going to want to see charts on my sheep?"

That gave him pause for reflection.

"Your dad?"

I shook my head.

"We can tack them on the stall walls and encourage all the animals to strive for greater performance," he grinned. "But first, you're going to have to teach the sheep to read left to right."

Basic computer systems function in a wonderfully dry, binary way. Either this or that, they say. That, you program. Either this or that, is the follow-up question. That, again. A lot of American farmers immediately saw the advantages of computers. They programmed lighting in the barns, feed onto conveyor belts into the pens, heating, watering, and so on. I've been in eighteenth-century barns outfitted with a wall of blinking lights and buttons that hum as they command the farm. Moreover, computers are more reliable than human beings when it comes to flipping switches at certain moments in the day. On a farm, this is a real consideration. Livestock appreciate routine almost as much as I do. Chickens respond dramatically to the steady number of daylight hours they receive. And as for heating, don't ever forget how forlorn pigs look when they shiver.

On farms that offer you the peak of technological performance systems, you can bet that the next barn over is likely a garage. It houses all those air-conditioned, stereo-accoutered, laser-guided, petroleum-quaffing tractors that rumble down the furrows with a princess's sensitivity and disposition to minor maladies. For me, this has crossed a technological line into something quite overwhelming and even a bit alienating. This is not the stuff of a small farm. The equipment you generally find lying about small farms has (a) probably been lying about for no inconsiderable time, and (b) may well have been purchased in a similarly shunned and modest condition. Small farms are modest, gerry-built. You're more apt to find wood than iron, on the pithy assumption that any fool can nail two pieces of pine together with the objective of effecting a stockade of sorts. Nothing looks really impregnable, but then the animals, too, generally have a less harassed air about them due to more liberal confinement systems and more relaxed routines.

On small farms, hay gets stacked in the barns neither with houndstooth precision nor to fantastic height. It has to be accessible. It can't soar to the rafters screaming out for an elaborate fire control system. The tractor ("It's somewhere outside, isn't it?") is a spindly-looking thing. Its skinny wheels sport no colorful hubcaps. It has no interior cab. From certain angles you can see through the engine to the corn fields beyond. When in action, with spiky attachments pinned to the rear axle, it rolls over the sod doing exactly what its high-tech cousins do—

ploughing, harrowing, cultivating, tilling, seeding, harvesting, whatever.

I tend to think that, whether you own a dinosaur Deere or the latest digitalized Dolby stereo tractor with all the works, farming is pretty much the same old job it always was. Until we finally move the planted acre into the laboratory and replace soil as the growing medium with agar gel in petri dishes, the farmer's job and struggles will continue to maintain their antique profile.

I once tried to convince an acquaintance that agriculture was fated to remain singularly embedded in its ancient roots; that one needs land, that ploughing, cultivating, seeding, and harvesting were the unavoidable staples of the trade.

This woman worked for an automobile-industry chemicals import firm. She didn't go along with that, she said. Farming, she felt, was no less modernized than any other business.

I said, the tools and machinery were updated, certainly, but the anatomy of the relationship of farmer to land and to nature was still quite unassuming, simple.

No way, she said. The farmer is a modern businessman with the constraints of all beltway businesses. He worries about things like Communism just like everyone else. He's got a telephone tie-up with the Chicago Board of Trade.

They don't trade lettuce on the CBOT, I murmured.

She added, Anyone can farm today, if they can read the label on fertilizer packages and drive a car. Actually, tractors are easier to drive than cars. It does make the point though. I mean, forget about seeds; the modern farmer is just another guy down the food chain that knows his income is somehow dependent on petroleum prices.

I thought, Yeah, just like a woman who fills out customs applications so that a car mechanic in Idaho can repaint a Honda four-door sedan with a chemically formulated tint of red that kills all life forms it inadvertently touches.

I said, These big guys can mechanize and computerize until

the whole world runs off one megabyte, but someone still has to plough up the dirt, drop an appropriate seed in it, react to rain, react to no more rain, and harvest at the right time.

If they can send monkeys into space, she said, they can teach monkeys to plough a field. I know. I've been to EPCOT.

6

Drugs and
Felicitous Bugs

One of the first questions people ask me when I mention my interest in starting a farm is: will I use chemicals? This line, delivered in varying intonations with raised eyebrows and miens of horror and condemnation, invariably leaves me flustered. I want to respond: Look, wait, this is a complicated subject and if you really want an answer, I'll need to back up a minute and give you some background and balance out your eminently evident predisposition. But usually I just say, gently, "I might."

Anyone who has ever had a garden, or tried to cultivate flowers, fruits, or vegetables, knows the agony of watching the foliage turn crusty brown, the leaves become lacy with holes, the stalks droop, the buds rot, the plants forcibly transposed from your own property to that of a robust colony of oddly striped beetles. You can be overwhelmed by a feeling of helplessness and gloom. It is with this in mind, that I muster a good deal of empathy for crop farmers in their impasses with insect, weed, and mineral depredations. I can see them reaching for their proverbial guns—and for the farmer, this refers to a virtual armory of undiluted chemical canisters stockpiled in the barn. Likewise, for farmers who witness their livestock listless from disease or depleted by parasites, there is an obliging arsenal of chemical—medicinal, pharmaceutical—remedies dispensed by the major drug houses or local veterinarians.

In instances such as these, I see the rationale behind the development of agricultural chemicals in a succinctly positive light; as part of the effort to keep stock healthy and fields unscourged. But development didn't stop there—and these days little in life is restrained from its potential for inborn extremisms—and the farm chemical industry marched on at full tilt to mature into a highly specialized array of soil conditioners, pest-specific insecticides, prophylactic feed supplements, synthesized anabolic steroids, apple ripeners, etc. So when I think about agricultural chemicals in general, and when I think about using them on my own farm, I find a thousand points of hesitation flooding into my brain.

"You can't just stop using chemical inputs," said one rancher to me. "They're integral to all farming industries now. Take out the chemicals, and the whole structure of the cattle business and the grain business and the cabbage business, for that matter— it'll just fall apart."

This perspective seemed to me a mix of resignation and boast. It echoed the sentiments of the whole American agricultural establishment, which appears to be aggressively wed to its chemical inputs with little opportunity for negotiation. Production agriculture would indeed undergo substantial structural changes with the elimination or reduction of many chemical inputs, just as it underwent immense change with the arrival and infusion and bloom of those chemical inputs in the first place—in the 1950s, the 1960s, and beyond. Is change so threatening, I wondered?

"Yes," said my husband. "Unfortunately."

I believe that much of the national farm lobby has affixed itself to the status quo of modern agriculture. So, gainfully, have the chemical and pharmaceutical lobbies. These groups share an interest in maintaining the current structure of farming—the dependence on man-made inputs, the monoculture, the densities of livestock feedlots—and they have become as expert in the art of politics as in the science of agriculture. They have given Congress and the American people a sense that there is no in-between—chemicals or no chemicals. But of course, there is an in-between, a kind of demilitarized zone of moderation that awaits some management and vision.

"Monarchies have their alluring aspects," my husband grinned at me as I was bristling about the poor agricultural leadership in America. "You could certainly effect change more quickly as a queen."

But could I, in fact? First, could I actually effect material changes in agriculture if granted monarchical powers for a period; and second, what would I try to change if I had the chance? The first question I quickly sized up as a philosophical morass. Having read Zhores Medvedev's book *Soviet Agriculture* (W. W. Norton, 1987), I did have the feeling that, though policies might change, peoples don't. So essentially, I didn't think that, even with a brief stint as agricultural potentate, I could execute or secure major changes in America's farm economy.

"Italy will always be anarchical," a friend once said to me, "and that's part of why it's so wonderful."

And Americans will likely cavort within the same capitalist, self-enriching ethic that arrived on the *Niña,* the *Pinta* and the *Santa Maria,* and which the authors of *The Federalist Papers* tried to rein in. So while I would hanker for the chance to revise a few of our agricultural policies—the crop price support programs or the antiquated milk pricing systems—I have a sense that the American pursuit of wealth and security would ultimately prevail. I could imagine the unfolding of events: I would cut one program, take a little of the federal welfare system out of agriculture, say, and immediately the congressional bureaucracy would well up around me with new, compensating legislation and support mechanisms, and wash away, like the waves, any hole I had dug in the sand.

As for the second question, about exactly what I would try to change, I think I would focus on the issue of chemical inputs to production agriculture. Here is where our American liberalism, in my mind, has given way to some serious abuses. Samuel Johnson once said: "Man's chief merit consists in resisting the impulses of his nature." I believe that when it came to farm chemicals, Americans did not resist the impulses of their natures. Chemical use in production agriculture has been excessive. I don't know anyone who would dispute it.

I telephoned my sister the doctor.

"Do you really wash all your fruit?" I asked with a whine that no doubt betrayed my own lethargic attitude.

"Yes," she said dogmatically.

"But is that enough then? Not all the chemicals are on the outside, you know. They get inside, too."

"Oh!" she sighed, tired from a day of hospital rounds. "Don't bother me with the details."

She said, "Are you reading those books again? Don't. It'll paralyze you."

My sister had spent a few years running a public health clinic in Osceola, Arkansas, on the bank of the Mississippi River. She lived in the midst of soybean country—in fact, one of America's biggest margarine moguls lived right down the street. My sister remembered vividly the many times she dealt with crop chemical emergencies.

"One day," she said, "they rushed an old man into my clinic who was driving down the main road while the farmers were all out in their yellow crop-dusting planes. He opened his window, he said, to get the bad smell out of the car. Heart attack. We have him in the intensive care unit for a week. He gets out of the hospital, he's driving down the main road again, this time on his way home—another plane. Smells bad. He opens his window. Heart attack.

"Apart from that, we got people all the time with their hands burned up from chemicals, funny cancers, kids with acute leukemia, families vomiting for days because they ate vegetables from their own gardens. . . . Nice business, these farm chemicals. Nobody needs to bother with a gun when you can buy poison at the supermarket."

She added, "So wash your fruit and vegetables."

Some days it seemed like the healthy tinge was draining out of farming as through a sieve. I never imagined having a farm that was large enough to warrant aerial dustings of pesticides or defoliants, but I hadn't completely ruled out the application of specific chemicals in my cropping, either.

"Just as a for-instance," I said to my sister, "getting away from the food angle. Supposing I had a farm, and supposing I were professionally trained to apply certain agricultural chemicals like pesticides, say, and supposing I wake up one day to this apocalyptic mealyworm infestation—don't you think it would be worth the risk to go out and spray? I mean, are the risks so high?"

"Yup."

This was sobering news indeed.

·

My husband is the ingredient-reader of the family. It's worthwhile not taking him to the drugstore. He's apt to stop dead in the aisle, somewhere between bunion remedies and shaving creams, his jaw dropped, reading the ingredients of my shampoo. It is mortifying.

I'll say, "Okay, okay, let's get along."

"I've only gotten through the nonactive ingredients," he will mumble, in shock.

I say, "Look, all shampoos are composed of the same stuff. People buy one or another for the scent."

He doesn't hear me. His head is shaking. This has deeply disturbed him. He looks down at his hands.

"I can't believe they haven't dissolved," he will whisper.

We live with an extraordinary amount of chemicals in our

day—on our scalp, in our food. I would rather not farm with chemicals, although I sometimes wonder, with today's apple and potato varieties, whether that's possible. So many fruits and vegetables have been bred to complement certain herbicides and pesticides.

My husband and I believe in a sustainable agriculture. We believe this world flirts with ever-larger Malthusian correctives, and we also think a farm run sensibly (in our mind, ethically), without a substantial chemical dependency, will be a satisfying challenge. Further, we will have the experiences of the last couple of decades to draw on in determining which methods of cultivation and irrigation are most successful, which grains provide how much protein, and what kinds of chemicals are least toxic, most effective, most readily applied, and so forth.

When I have spoken to farmers about circulating proposals for "environmentally friendly" agricultural practices, they have often responded contemptuously or defensively. Many felt assaulted by the first wave of environmentalist fervor rather than courted by the kinder, gentler, and potentially profitable new methods of operation. Many, in their tucked flannel shirts and chemical-company-issue baseball caps, felt they were being preached to by a body of environmentalists, Native Americans, and first-time East Coast mothers. What did this coalition know about farm economics? And that describes in good part the controversy. Proponents of chemical-free agriculture are battling for chemical-free food. Farmers are battling for their livelihood. You can't win arguments when you're arguing about different issues.

I don't side with the farmers necessarily. I, too, like my food to arrive without warning labels. But there's a particular facet of the farmer-chemical subject that piques my interest. It's little discussed because there's essentially no such profession as agrosociology. And thank goodness.

I think that what wedded farmers to farm chemicals (apart from the latter's effectiveness, convenience, and economics) was that chemicals affirmed them as members of a modern-age professional culture. The people from Dow and Dupont and Monsanto gave farmers a new kind of stature, addressed them like honorary scientists, distinguished them in new four-color trade journals, scooped them up from the dusts of Oklahoma and posited them in the ranks of mutual fund stockholders—the au courant of today's financial bystanders. Computer technologies, following on the heels of the chemical revolution, plopped fittingly into this new professional lap.

It's a question of image, which for most people runs deeper than rationale. As for me, I shirk this image of the modern farmer. I don't want to feel a kinship with everyone who chooses office work and watches reruns of "Dallas." I prefer windows that open, heat in summer, and cold in winter. If farm chemicals were my bridge to the corporate experience, I would definitely turn them down. Even so, I have a compassion for the other side, the desire of the erstwhile Okie to reach for a higher stature.

How alike we will all soon become, I sometimes think.

So, there will be little or no chemicals on my farm. I shall try to be clever and resourceful. We have read up a lot on integrated pest management (IPM) principles, whereby benchmarks of infestations must be reached before any retaliatory action is needed. I'll couple this with crop rotations—corn one year, for example, barley the next, carrots the next, and back to corn. Crop rotation prevents the entrenchment of pests particularly keen on certain crops. It is a simple strategy and it's even suggested for your backyard garden. The experts will tell you: Never never plant your broccoli in the same place in consecutive years.

I'm also keeping informed about the positive and time-tested results from "biological controls." Biological control piggybacks on nature's own habits of predation. But who do you call? I wonder. No one is listed in the yellow pages under "Sale and Spraying of Sterilized Male Cutworms," or "Procurement of Suppressing Bugs and Natural Enemies." Moreover, there are a few biological remedies I would like to be protected from myself—blackflies, for instance, and I don't care if they are partial to aphids.

In New England, many rural properties are equipped with bat houses because bats adore eating mosquitoes and don't bother people, much. One Connecticut farmer I met kept a flock of guinea hens on his land because he said they ate the ticks that carried Lyme Disease. These control systems may have a limited efficacy. They may also have their charmless repercussions. Too many bats hanging around, so to speak. Too many fat black flies for your liking. Too many frogs once the flies are gone, and so forth. Keep the cycle going, and you'll recreate the plagues of Job in your own backyard.

·

The conspicuous alternative to using agricultural chemicals, in a black and white world, is to farm organically. No broadly accepted definitions exist in the trade to help the budding farmer understand exactly what categorizes certifiably organic practices. Facing this void, I have felt the best thing to do as part of my investigation was to speak with organic farmers and nonorganic farmers, and to clarify my own sentiment regarding organic and nonorganic food. Food is, for many people, the conclusive issue.

"I dun like the extra chores," said one organic farmer from Pennsylvania to me. "But I cannuh eat ta other."

The term "organic farming" encompasses a set of crop and animal husbandry practices that rely on naturally occurring inputs to production (no man-made chemicals), and that seem to emphasize the replenishment of the soil in an ecologically sound way. Composting, mulching, and the use of natural fertilizers, herbicides, insecticides, and fungicides, are considered the three fundamental and interrelated building blocks of organic farming. When organic farmers need to apply nitrogen to their soils, they look to such mineral-rich sources as blood meal, cottonseed meal, fish meal, and manure. They may mulch the ground between crop rows with newspaper or wood chips to suppress weed growth, or they may hoe. Wood ash, they know, will supply their soil with needed potassium. Marigolds, with varying degrees of reliability, are expected to deflect nematodes, and so on.

Organic farming suits people who feel a particular way about their land and their food. It puts farmers in closer touch with the spontaneous regeneration of their soil, the palpable vitality of their foliage, or the natural resilience of their animals. These farmers choose to work very intimately with the natural cycles and paces of their plants and livestock. They try to find within nature the nourishment or predatory checks that keep a barnyard healthy. This approach is philosophically at odds with the methods of most modern, larger-scale nonorganic farmers, who customarily depend upon the efficacy of chemical inputs to provide their soils with vital nutrients, their plants with blanket protection, and their animals with boosted vigor. Moreover, nonorganic farmers I have visited tend to maintain that corn is corn, meat is meat, and food is food is food. Organic farmers, alternatively, seem to look more dotingly on their produce, to encounter within each orange or zucchini the miraculous universe of the aboriginal seed. There is a sense of pride among many organic farmers I have met, that their yields are derived without artificial means. Does organic produce truly taste better than nonorganic produce, or even different? Is it worth the typically higher cost? These are among the fiercely disputed controversies of the field.

A couple of years ago, I had the opportunity to visit with a celebrated chef from the Plaza Hotel at a luncheon that featured only natural, or organic, foods. He looked up at me from some delicately seasoned flageolets and said, "You know, the problem I have with this organic food stuff is that only the rich can afford it."

Everyone at our table looked down at his or her plate. Yes, there was an all-organic spinach pasta at five times the price of a regular box of durum noodles. It was coiled attractively next to a portion of pond-raised salmon flown in, we were told, from Washington State's "spring-pure" waters at a cost that would make one faint. The meal was to be accented with a champagne from vines untouched by human chemicals, and a salad of miniature vegetables adoringly sprouted without the aide of fertilizers, pesticides, fungicides, or other zesty toxins.

As we nibbled appreciatively on this kingly fare, we were treated to "a few words" from more than a few people in the organic food industry. We might have to pay a little extra, they told us, but natural, chemical-free foods were worth it. They were better for the environment and better for us. They were going to become, these spokesmen said, the new gourmet foods of America. The Plaza chef turned to me.

"Bean sprouts of the rich and famous," he said with some derision.

America spends less of its income on food than any other country in the world. Our food is cheap—that's always been the goal of the USDA—and its quality ranks among the highest anywhere. Things were pretty dandy until the 1980s, when our intensifying national preoccupation with health and diet induced us to make top-gun scientists of nutritionists and other food interpreters. Immediately, eggs went down in a blaze of fat and cholesterol. Beef was crippled by early allegations of its intimate association with heart attacks. Pesticide residues, it seemed, were turning up by the teaspoonful on every green leaf and grape. It was like a period of McCarthyism in the supermarket, only the villain this time was not Communism, but rather our country's mainstream agricultural dogma. In the midst of this fever, organic farming logically thrived.

It was a new generation of organics this time, however, a shade more sophisticated than the 1970s variety. Natural food stores turned into hot properties. They became chic, well-lit, well-stocked, and staffed by clean and knowledgeable clerks. This time around, organic foods were very à la mode. Blood oranges replaced regular oranges. Purple peppers replaced the traditional green ones. Such a trendy approach to food retailing appealed to new audiences, particularly to young and affluent professionals who had become even more discriminating about their intake and bored with the usual fare. Why eat green beans, after all, when you can simmer those diamond-hard little flageolets for six hours?

Meanwhile, the news media inundated our television screens and nonrecycled front pages with stories of environmental damage done to natural resources by agricultural enterprises. A dirge was sung for the Chesapeake Bay. Cattle relieving themselves of gas, discreetly or not, were indicted for furthering the destruction of the earth's protective ozone. We were all encouraged to "eat natural," but the truth was, we couldn't all afford it. Food stamps, for instance, don't go a long way on organic fruits and vegetables. So some people worried about whether we had essentially relegated low-income populations to low-quality food.

I don't think so. The American food supply—organic and nonorganic together—continues to rank in a category of premium quality. Chemical use is stringently regulated in this country, in spite of exaggeration to the contrary. Furthermore, it's highly unregulated in most developing populations throughout the world (to whom we continue to export our most lethal agricultural toxins, and from whom we continue to import produce; so, well, okay). Many agricultural specialists believe that it was because chemical use could not be sufficiently policed in Europe that the EEC banned used of livestock hormones altogether.

America's poor, through welfare programs designed to maximize their independence, are in fact in a position to consume high-value foods—breads, pastas, vegetables, fruits, milk, cheese, poultry, and so on. I gather, however, that food stamp purchases persistently reflect preferences for low-value foods—potato chips, candy, soda—and for foods that are relatively expensive: frozen dinners, for example, or precooked canned entrées and side dishes. This leads me to believe that lousy nutrition among America's lower classes is not simply a failing of food stamps or a problem of poor-quality foodstuffs, but rather a more profound issue involving education, employment, and our welfare system.

All said, the chef from the Plaza had a valid point. Organic food is considerably more expensive than nonorganic food—largely because it costs more to produce. It requires more labor, as it did in the old days, to cultivate one's organic furrow. It takes more time to check for and do battle with insects, and people are less efficient than aerial dustings of poison in dispatching bugs or weeds. Moreover, organic methods often yield less per acre than pumped-up, super-fertilized vegetables or correspondingly pumped-up, super-fed animals.

Organic farms also sacrifice many of the conveniences of large-scale nonorganic farming. For instance, because insects will prosper in the monoculture of vast, single-cropped acreage, organic farms seem to manage best if the terrain is divided into relatively small plots, perhaps only one-quarter acre in size, with crops interspersed among one another, and with all crops rotated year after year. This tends to render impractical most modern farm equipment, whose complex systems of adjustment and navigation become extremely clumsy in the compact and diverse plots. Some experimental technologies are currently emerging to allow for large-scale organic monoculture. These have included: the industrial vacuuming of insects from crop rows; searing fields with tightly controlled flame jets just above plant height; and crop dusting with hoppers full of good bugs ready to eat the bad bugs. Such new technologies are gradually being refined, but may still suffer the disadvantages of high energy cost, ground compaction, the inadvertent decimation of good as well as bad bugs—not to mention an occasional charring of the foliage.

·

"What's your view on organic produce?" I asked my father.

"Well, I think I do prefer the idea of organic," he said. "On the other hand, I realize it's sometimes impractical. Sometimes soils are so depleted that I expect you need to use chemical supplements to regenerate them. As for taste or cooking, I can't tell the difference."

A lot of the small farms in the Northampton area, farms whose stands now form the bulk of my father's Saturday morning farmers' market, are organic. When I shop with him, I notice that all the farmers are young, as though it's a whole new generation taking up and redefining the region's agriculture. It is heartening to see younger farmers at all these days—one of our nation's most serious agricultural concerns is that the majority of our farmers are nearing retirement, with only a meager legion of younger farmers ready to succeed them. Indeed, this void has in itself contributed to a quicker pace of decline in farm numbers. Elderly farmers, seeing no interested successor emerge from either their families or their communities, have more readily accepted buyout offers from real estate developers and government production-reduction programs, such as the 1985 Farm Bill's dairy herd buyout.

"I'm thinking back a minute," said my father. "I think I was first introduced to the idea of organic farms when we lived in Stockbridge in the 1950s. A woman next door came over one day and gave us a puppy. She insisted that we only feed it milk from an organic dairy farm across the border in New York State. Well, we thought she was just crazy."

"Crazy?" said an organic dairy farmer to whom I related this story. "Well, he was probably right. She probably was. And me, too. You gotta be nuts to go into the milk business, and completely wacko to do it organically." Which he himself had done. "Well, I did. And the reason being," he said, "because my wife here wants to sell organic veal. And I'll tell you, you can get a fine premium for organic veal in the markets now, but you canna get nothing fine for organic milk—in fact, I think folks shy away from organic milk a little to tell you the truth. I think when it comes to milk, folks prefer their cartons extra-bleached-out white, double and triple homogenized, if you catch my meaning.

"So I say, okay, to my wife, then I'm gonna hafta make this a kosher dairy, acause organic alone wull not pay me for my troubles. Rabbis in black nightgowns and the whole nine yards. And she just looked at me, jaw-dropped and all. And then she said, okay. And you can get a mighty fair premium for kosher milk nowadays, us being next to the New York City markets especially. We allays got a couple of rabbis living up in that trailer on the hill, and they're nice enough folk. Not too talkative, if I may say."

This farmer told me the biggest obstacle he faced in going organic was raising and procuring organic feeds for his dairy cattle. The first couple of years without chemicals, his pasture was poorer. His cost for supplemental organic feed corn was over thirty percent higher than in earlier years, before the switch to organic. He had to hire two extra men part-time to help him with the chores, because without the facility of chemicals, plant and animal health required more personally involved care. His bill for fertilizers, pesticides and herbicides, however, had dropped to nil.

"It's a funny thing," he said. "In the beginning I thought, by God, I'll never last. I wull lose this farm. But. It dunna whork that way finally. It whorks out fine. Ya couldn't pay me enough to go back to chemicals."

Some people seem to think that a lot of farmers switch to organic simply to capture the financial premiums accorded to all-natural produce, but I think it's clear that the extra hard work involved in organic farming would push to the limits anybody's endurance, patience, and greed. In many ways, "going organic" is going back to the early, labor-intensive practices of farming. It means you gather, haul, and spread that wet, stinky, heavy manure on your fields instead of reaching for the handy dusting gun. It means you get the hoe out, and not the blue canister of herbicide (anyone who has hoed knows well the tedium and muscle strain that herbicides promise to relieve). And for some people, going organic means you sell that eight-year-old Deere tractor and buy, for more money than that Deere netted you, a pair of Norwegian fjord draught horses plus the hardly run-of-the-mill paraphernalia that correctly links them with any farm equipment—harrow, plough, etc. After all, if you intend to farm organically, doesn't it imply that tractors are out? Wouldn't the exhaust and inevitable oil drips nullify your otherwise impeccably noncontaminating methods? The jury is out.

"I could envision using draught horses on the farm instead of a tractor," I mused one day to my husband.

"That's an interesting idea," he said.

Then he said, "You know, they're pretty big animals."

"You think they would be too expensive to feed?" I asked.

"I mean big—tall," he said. "A lot taller than you. Do you think you could sling the reins and yoke and everything over their heads?"

"It might take some doing," I smiled. "They'll have to be very good-natured. Do horses have senses of humor?"

On a small-scale farm, I think I would enjoy using draught horses at least some of the time, regardless of whether I farmed strictly organically or not. It would be a part of the pleasure of farming—part of the pure pleasure and part (remember that tractors are the alternative) of the quiet. There are other aspects of organic agriculture that strike me as definitely less agreeable. Among the worst is having to endear yourself to a host of insects. All farmers need some smattering of basic entomology in order to distinguish the good bugs of the farm world from the bad. Organic farmers, however, commonly cultivate populations of preferred bugs in order to obliterate (naturally) a menacing community of the bad. There are hoards of books and a few magazines that can help to guide you in this effort—not to mention the brink-of-extinction breed of County Extension Agents whose entomological colleagues are ably trained to provide assistance—but literature may be far less appealing than insecticides when you notice a blushing infestation of ravenous beetles shredding your tomato field.

For me, a prospective farmer with an environmentally conscientious nature, one of the biggest obstacles to organic farming has always been the proponents—the holier-than-thou or overly folksy timbre of their literature and arguments. I once bought my husband a subscription to *Organic Gardening* magazine, and the manner of many articles irritated us even when the information was useful. One article, a "Guide to Beneficial Insects" (May/June 1991), began with this childlike dramatization:

> The aphid with the amazing appetite may have finally run out of luck. A delicate green lacewing and its ugly, ravenous larva seem to be glancing in its direction!
>
> No, the larva is either unseeing or full, and the pretty parent is flying away on those glistening emerald wings. The aphid begins to let out a tiny bug sigh, but stops as an even more tenacious foe, the armored ladybug, hovers into view!
>
> In a blind panic, the aphid scampers away as quickly as its stubby little bug legs will carry it. Just a little further, it thinks, and it will be safely hidden . . .

Exclamation points and tiny bug sighs aside, I just don't like being talked to that way. I support organic agriculture but I don't identify in the least with the readers and writers of that magazine.

The above-threatened aphid, after an extended and melodramatic flight, bought it, as they say—*"CHOMP!"*—which is from my perspective a positive ending for the story, although it doesn't quite work the magic of making me disposed to buy cartons full of praying mantis eggs and predatory thrips—the militialike insecticides of the organic farmer. I would hasten to add, moreover, that a good thrip in the eyes of one farmer may be a threat to the crops of another farmer. This kind of complication is not what I would want to cultivate on my small farm.

I once worked alongside a young woman who was an ardent organic gardener, and she found enchantment in hatching lady-bugs (widely considered good bugs) and sprinkling diatomaceous earth on her plot of summer vegetables.

Diatomaceous earth, she explained to me, was a fine dust made from the shells of millennia-old one-celled diatoms. Insects and worms ingest it, and its silica structure wreaks havoc on their respiratory and digestive systems, ripping up their mini-ature internal tracts and at least maiming if not killing them. The image was enough to make me side with the bugs. I won-dered if someone had told the animal rights' people about this all-natural powder.

"Very effective," the woman said, nodding her head knowingly.

"It sounds it," I grinned. "No skull and crossbones on the side of the jar?"

What's a nice girl like you doing savaging these bugs? I thought.

·

I had heard that diatomaceous earth and bug therapies have been successfully used on organic farms of considerable size, but I wasn't sure that I could wholly embrace this kind of agriculture myself. I went to visit an organic farmer near Salisbury, Con-necticut, in the northwest corner of the state ("It's not hard to find; you'll see a fork in the road, take that left, keep driving till you see a green barn—that's ours . . ."), to learn about his methods and their proficiency.

"Fine, glad to have you come by," he had said over the tele-phone. "We just got recertified by the team from Cornell, so we're in good spirits here, too."

This was a gorgeous old farm, nestled in the bottomlands of a Berkshire foothills valley. It had belonged to the family of this man's in-laws for hundreds of years, and he had finally left his job as a science professor to farm it himself. Organic farms don't look different than nonorganic farms. I pulled up to the usual sights: an old barn painted green and hankering for some simple repairs, a couple of tractors left to rust outside, tires flung about, layers of cobwebs like cottony felt across the chicken wire of a small chicken coop, broken stairs leading to the lower floor of the barn, small paddocks of curious geometries, and the smell of fresh manure. Mr. Keats walked out of the darkness of the barn to greet me. He wore a bandanna over his head, and on top of that a straw hat. It was a hot summer day, but even in trousers and a long-sleeved shirt he seemed to be staying cool.

"Hello there," he said, holding out his hand for a warm hand-shake. "Keats. Glad to meet you. I'm afraid I don't have too much time today. We've got to get haying, you know, but let me show you around a bit."

We walked into his barn. It was built on a small hillside so that, depending on the direction you were coming from, there was a ground-level entrance into one of two floors. From the street side, we entered the main chamber of the barn. A tractor sat idle in the shadows. A table with a picnic cooler stood by the door and a cardboard sign leaned against the cooler indicating fresh eggs inside for sale: "Please leave one dollar per dozen." A chicken coop had been built into the far corner, and the resident hens and ducks intensified their workaday pandemonium in response to my unannounced appearance. Keats showed me a well-charged electric wire he had strung at the foot of the coop's fence.

"I was forced to," he said. "Have you ever dealt with raccoons? They are unbelievably persistent—I am tempted to say astute. Every night, it seemed, they would get into my coop and make off with a few birds. I would come in the morning and find holes cut in the wire—in the *wire*—or barn boards wrenched up just enough to let them in. No fence was high enough. They were single-handedly destroying my barn. And I'll tell you something else: Raccoons are not nice to find. You don't actually want to catch them red-handed unless you're good with a gun, which I'm not, but I'm getting there."

He kicked the wire and a sizeable spark jumped out.

"This works all right," he said. "It doesn't kill anybody, but it's a discouraging shot. Watch yourself down these steps," he said, and he led us down to the dark and cool lower level where he kept his cattle.

There was great variety down there. Guernsey. Hereford. Jersey. A Scotch Highland steer. A few pigs. Two new Holstein calves. A young Angus bull. The bull immediately sauntered over to us and I really felt the hairs on the back of my neck tingle. I tried to hide my terror but it must have been plain in my facial contortions.

"Don't be frightened," Keats smiled, scratching the furry black forehead of this stout bull. A short chain hung down from the bull's nose ring and swayed as the animal nuzzled Keats's side. "I raised this fellow myself, from the bottle up. It's a myth that you can't leave bulls loose, can't enjoy them this way. People just treat them so poorly—then they end up with a nasty-tempered animal. It's no surprise. It's the same with human beings."

We walked past his pig pens. I could hear the jingle of the nose ring and chain following behind us. I was so busy trying to pretend I didn't that I don't remember a thing about Keats's pigs. I think they were mostly pink Yorkshires, big and with erect ears. And there was one spotted Poland China, a smaller pig with black and gray spots on a white hide. We parted from the jingle by dint of a charged wire fence and entered an area of the lower barn that Keats had earmarked for grain and silage storage.

"Now here's a good illustration of farm life," he said. "I'm no wizard. When I decided to make my own silage I bought a few books, took it all in, tried it out—nothing. Rotten, over-fermented nothing. So I experimented for a few years with more or less moisture, different ingredients, until I got a good mixture for myself. My mix probably wouldn't work well for the next fellow, but it's perfect here. Now I don't even think about it.

"Farming's not so hard. There aren't any mysteries. You have to blunder through this or that aspect, but then you don't again. I've got lousy land here," he waved toward the valley beyond the barn. "We flood almost every year. It looks beautiful today because we're in the midst of a terrific drought, but normally one-half of my land is a swamp." He smiled. "So you do what you can. You farm here and there. You switch varieties. You seed a new meadow. What's wonderful about farming is that it's open to your tailoring. No hard rules. You scrap along with new ideas, you buy another used tractor from another guy going out of the business, you find baby lambs on your doorstep one morning from the farmer down the road. The only hard piece of advice I have for you is not to run out and overcapitalize yourself. Start simple. Things come your way. A lot of farmers in this area will tell you the same thing—in all their years they've never bought a new tractor."

We walked outside and watched the Canadian geese wander freely through the cattle pasture picking undigested bits of corn from the manured ground. I realized that, for midsummer, Keats's black fly problem was very low. This piqued my interest, because I sometimes wonder whether black flies are the one central obstacle standing between me and my farm. I hate them.

"Nice of you to notice," Keats said when I mentioned the flies. "Well, we work at it. We keep moving our manure. We try to keep it dry, spread, less of a breeding ground. I used to buy traps but I haven't found a one that really solves the problem. I keep a few still in the barn, to relieve the animals. Me, I've gotten used to the flies at this level. But we have our house up on that hill across the valley, so we're fortunate not to live directly beside them. My wife would curse them in the house."

"Does your wife help on the farm?" I asked.

"No, she works in town, and she takes care of our daughter.

Taking care of our daughter is full-time work in itself," he laughed. "But she's a spinner, too, and a weaver, so she makes things from our wool—place mats, scarves—that we sometimes sell at the farmers' markets.

"Farming's a habitual life, but it's an individual thing—you make your own routines. It can be lonely, too, depending upon your impression of animals. I find great interest and amusement in animals, and I would say that after fighting in Vietnam, and after years of Peace Corps work in China, I find civilization a thin veneer. Human beings are not so far from other animals as we like to believe."

He looked up at me to see if I would be surprised, but I wasn't. I also think that "civilization" must be constantly aspired to, and that human beings come gutturally close to mimicking the brutality or pure dumbness of many other animals. Are the incidents of destructive ferocity between modern-day nations or tribes any less barbaric than intraspecies violence in the wild? Is there an animal that shows itself as small-minded and preening as America's Senate Judiciary Committee? (Just consider the Clarence Thomas Supreme Court nomination hearings.) When I am herded onto an airplane, am I shuffled forward with any more dignity than a cow?

"Livestock," I said to Keats, "at least don't have pretenses of a more genteel breeding. They're probably less introspective, but I don't find them less gracious than many people on the street."

Keats laughed. He said, "I find great satisfaction here." And he cast a long look across his valley, from the far hill where he kept sheep, to an old shade tree in the field under which several cattle were resting, and over to his brand-new towering navy blue silo that seems like a modern day badge of success for farmers nationwide. "Even in our toughest times, in the early days of righting this crumbling old farm, I found a great peace in the raw chores. In farming, your aspirations have to be within the chores themselves. You have to want to work with and be interested by the earth, when it's mud, when it's ice, when it's swamp, or when it's wildflowers. It's not nearly as comfortable or lucrative as my school job was. I sometimes have to remind my friends of that—these are people who earn hundreds of thousands of dollars every year in banking or business and who think my way of life seems somehow preferable. Well, it is preferable to me. But I don't think they'd like it very much, not at all.

"It's very humbling, farming is. You find there's not a lot a man can bring to it all, other than some management. Animals are pretty capable when it comes to taking care of themselves, and frankly, without us they'd probably have evolved into better specimens than they are today.

"A small farmer like me doesn't grow tired of the basic miracles of seeds and newborn calves. Sure, I get tired of waking up at three a.m. every Saturday morning to drive to the New York City farmers' market, but I don't get bored with my work here on the other days. I'm never indifferent to the growth of plants, the way hay dries, the interactions of these animals. A farmer sees miracles right in front of himself. I'm not religious, and I probably shouldn't use the word *miracle*—but farmers I know are just open to the wonderment of it all. It's nice, that, in such a jaded society."

I spent a couple of hours with Keats, who, I learned, had been a Harvard graduate within a distinguished family of "Princeton men" before settling on this old farm. It explained his eloquence, of course. And it ratified for me, in my own language, my own choice.

·

I had a close brush with organic agriculture when we lived in Connecticut. I took an opportunity to work for a small farm business that produced gourmet, specialty, all-natural organic meats—beef, primarily, but some chicken, too. It was a family operation, heavily subsidized by inherited family money and entirely run according to puzzling family ethics. The "husbandry" was founded on a singular mixture of ancient Chinese nutritional theory, a handful of American Indian iconologies, and ultramodern computer systems. Unfortunately, while these unusual building blocks were always chatted up with a kind of conceit—the pride of knowing who among mankind was and is actually right about everything—they had never quite been put into service during the several years before I arrived, during my tenure there, or thereafter.

In the beginning I used to say to myself, "Well, some people are more patient than I when it comes to effecting their dreams." Later I grew more suspicious. It was an instructive if disheartening experience for me. The owner of this beef operation was terribly rich, and one might rightly suppose, "Ah, then you truly can afford to execute this elaborate plan, because the money it will cost is astounding." But sometimes it is the rich who have the most trouble making life real, realized.

The meat from this farm was organic and it was not. It was organic because the cattle and chickens were fed no medicated feeds, injected with no steroids, and otherwise cloistered from veterinary care. Indeed, these livestock were fattened on things like garlic, sweet potatoes, and dandelion greens—things it was difficult even to call fodder, livestock fodder. How much more natural can it get than to have cattle rely upon garlic bulbs for their unfailing health?

Well, in fact this operation was never and would never be certified organic by the prevailing self-appointed certifying bodies of the time, because the feeds used were not certified organic feeds. The sweet potatoes came waxed and dirty from the Carolinas via the Bronx's notorious Hunt's Point Market. The garlic came from Chile, California, wherever. The other greens, a confidential composition of sure-to-surprise-you grasses and vegetables and fruits, also came from regular market channels. This is taboo among organic circles, where feeds must be verified organic for the ultimate meat to be called organic.

For me, these lapses in orthodox organic statute are no major issue. I'm wishy-washy enough about most food-related fetishes that any faux pas committed along the extremist fringe don't rattle me. The meat from this farm was delicious, normally, if entirely inconsistent. And if the hay had been grown with fertilizers, it didn't matter to me. If the garlic came from South America, no problem. No problem for me, I should clarify, but once a severe problem for several hundred chickens. One truckload of particularly piquant Chilean garlic, I was told, devastated the combined intestines of the chicken coop for a week.

While I worked for this tiny beef company, I rubbed shoulders with organic enthusiasts and those who went along with the organic party line ("It's a job"). It was a community in which radical and emotional convictions about pure and unadulterated foods were the accepted cant. There was a kind of shrillness to the argument, I felt. It reminded me of being in a movie theatre: at first the sound system booms extremely loud, bites into you, and you think you will not last the whole film—and then you acclimate. After a few months of working in the organic foods realm, I became inured to the din of the partisan throng.

I had not just taken a job, however, I had bumped into a way of life, an ideology every bit as bullying as . . . as every other ideology. Everyone needed a water purifier (did I mean to drink bilge?), no one could eat veal (did I know where that came from?), and bodies were naturally temples. I was inundated with propaganda detailing the good, labyrinthine processes of organic food production versus the bad and less labyrinthine processes of our drug-addicted modern agriculture. One of the aspects I found most nettling was an underlying accusation that nonorganic farmers were lazier, always looking to take the easy route out with regard to everything from field tilth to plant yield to livestock viruses.

All told, I remain an ally of organic farmers, who, as it often happens, tend not to be themselves the kind of fringe activists that their industry lobbyists would have you believe. Fresh spirit was breathed into the organic food business at the end of the 1980s, and I think it has proven to be a healthy thing because it has brought new voices and persuasions into a fairly traditional industry. How far I take the organic principles on my own farm will only be determined over time. After all, I'm married to a man who maintains that the person who invented sour-cream-and-onion-flavored potato chips deserved a Nobel prize in chemistry. We are not witlessly chemical-averse.

My husband and I both believe in setting up a farm on a pragmatic basis and taking nonchemical measures as far as we reasonably can, but we don't want to sacrifice our crops and stock to the organic cause. We need to be coldly realistic—take in everybody's propaganda and vilify it all. We are loath to engage in chemical warfare against the ground and its bugs, out of the same subconscious aversion we have to taking pills—not a particularly reasoned response, but firmly felt. The hazards inherent in the application of insecticides, and our awareness that residues survive and survive in every clump of dirt or feeding trough, have gone a long way toward persuading us that some organic methods are worth a try.

We know a couple from New York City who grow apples espalier-style on their estate in Long Island. Well, it is the husband alone that cultivates the perfect tendrils and fruiting. Every weekend he can be found out on their Hamptons lawn, having molted his tailored suits, snipping and spraying away in a roomy coverall and work boots. He drags tanks, sacks, and spray-guns of chemicals happily between the rows of his leafing artistry, dousing the foliage much as one might retouch a painting. His wife, however, who worries for the health of their children and their two short-legged dogs, is threatening to buy a separate washing machine for the exclusive purpose of detoxifying his gardening clothes. She cannot bear the bags and canisters of fungicides, fertilizers, and pesticides that lie stacked in their garage.

"Can't you do this without chemicals?" she once asked him.

"Isn't there such a thing as organic espalier?" I piped up.

And he replied theatrically, as though quoting Shakespeare, "Nope."

I hope I am not so tied to the market basket of agricultural chemicals when I start my farm. Still, insect infestations and fungus spread may indeed pressure me into reconsideration. And where I do already and fervently see the need for a chemist's hand is in the occasional treatment of unhealthy animals—in pharmaceuticals. It is painful for me to think of orthodox organic farmers who stint on the comfort and treatment of their animals in sickness. I wouldn't play around with herbal remedies if a ewe or kid were taken ill. I would call the doctor.

"So," I said to my father one afternoon. He was busy tying the drooping limbs of his frail six-foot Japanese maple to the fence behind it. He had gotten a little discouraged when an itinerant goldfinch landed on one of the branches for a rest, and the branch had bowed, bowed, bowed down to the ground with this added weight. "A candidate for some injectable mineral pith-acceleration supplements?"

"Hmmm," he sighed. He seemed pretty demoralized. "Maybe I'll go to Agway and see what they've got. Does Agway have an emergency ward?"

"It's not that bad," I said. "It's adolescence, gawky adolescence."

"If you weren't around," he said, "I'd pull out my big guns."

"Big guns?"

"Japanese maple steroids," he teased.

"You've got me all wrong, Dad. I'm undecided on the organic orthodoxy. I'm trying to find out where the balance of sensibility lies. Who knows? I may be Miss Medicine Cabinet in the year 2000. I may have your Japanese maple hooked to an intravenous protein drip."

"Oh, I know that," he said. He did.

He mixed some Miracle Gro into a watering pail and splashed the base of the tree. The trunk was as thick as my wrist and my heart went out to him. What could be done? I would certainly not be so pious as to swear off fertilizers in the face of such a tree.

"So," I said. "Are you going to come over to the farm now and then and give my guys a shot of penicillin?"

"Natch," he said. He set down the watering pail. "And you, too."

Part Three

Tender

7

Orchards, Groves, and Furrows

If you take Route 66 out of Northampton, due west, you run quickly into farmland that has been converted into suburban neighborhoods. That must surely be the refrain of the 1990s—a mass lament for memories of open space and wilderness that we all still have and that our children will not know. I hope my children, when they are thirty, will be saying: "You know, Mom, that valley used to be filled with tasteless homes and swimming pools, and now it's all prairie." It sounds inane. It would only work, anyway, if I and everyone else *didn't have* children, if the population of our world were to shrink to sound numbers and humanity could take hold again.

Route 66 was piney, twisting, and exciting—so perceived from my ever-alert traffic control station in the backseat—for its steep hills. During the warmer months, my mother would pack us four girls, aged four to twelve, into the car and we would head out along the bumpy road for an expedition. Twenty minutes would get us to Clear Falls, a lovely lake that has since become private because of all the buses that began to turn up. Thirty minutes took us to Outlook Farm, where they used to grind up peanut butter as we watched and where fresh-cured hams and slabs of white bacon hung from the ceiling. (It's quite different now, since the USDA began cracking down on such homespun establishments; today Outlook Farm will sell you stinky potpourris and quaintly packaged jams from God knows where.) Forty minutes would find us at Lake Norwich, where we fished along the silty bottoms, baiting our stick-and-twine rods with scraps of yellow napkin. We used to catch little golden sunfish by the dozens, carefully liberating them from our hooks with a cautionary scolding not to fall for yellow napkins again. It was no doubt during these summers that I acquired my un-limited lack of respect for fish. And so, while aquaculture is nowadays an accepted segment of agriculture, you won't find mention of Tilapia fry tanks in any index of mine.

The first part of Route 66 was always the same. We passed woods, horses, cows, apple orchards, hay fields, and an old chicken house. We four nondrivers bounced up and down on the worn seat springs of the station wagon as we drove over the wells and dips of the pavement. We got to love the familiar sights along this road, our landmarks, ticking them off one by one, and announcing competitively which the next would be. The most harrowing part of the trip came when, after curling through the shadowy hollow of a pine grove, we would suddenly find ourselves hurtling downhill at a rate of thirty miles an hour toward a tiny stone bridge that we knew would only fit one station wagon. Ours. *Waaaaaah!* came the hysteria from the backseats. Did our mother want us all killed?

Sometimes I drove out with my mother to pick up my older sisters after their horseback riding lessons. The lessons were held in an old barn full of big cats with a fortunately benign dis-position. I loved cats, and they seemed like especially good playmates for a four-year-old who was not much bigger than they when everybody was standing tall on two legs. It was never easy to chase one down, however; they must have had a different sense of what playing with me would be like. So I would usually get some assistance in the catching—one of the riding teachers would settle a miserable gray tom into my ready, affectionate hug—and I would take it for a walk to see the horses with my arms clasped tight around its shoulders, its front paws squeezed into a limp X in front of its face, its back legs dangling down to my red Mary Janes. Even today I remember those barn cats with both a child's happy zeal and an adult's apology. When I see a little child trying to cradle a cat or small dog, I am amazed at the animal's forgiving grit as its limbs are pulled and twisted and heartily reorganized to gain a better purchase. Cats must have very versatile stomach compartments.

One day, as we were driving out to the horse barn, my mother stopped the car by the roadside and stepped out. She smelled the air and smiled broadly.

"How would you like to pick strawberries?" she said to me.

Strawberries. What an adventure, I thought. Wouldn't I have something to tell my sisters. I bundled out of the car while my mother produced, magically, two bowls from our kitchen. From our kitchen! I thought, now this is really something dazzling. We walked up a small incline into a rolling meadow. The grass disappeared suddenly, no longer tickling my legs, and I looked down. Bright red tiny strawberries were bobbing everywhere under green leaves.

"Here's a bowl for you to put your berries in," said my mother. She spread out a blanket from the car. "Strawberries can be pretty prickly. If it stings, you can sit on this."

They were wild strawberries we picked—tiny, each the size of a little fingernail, growing like a dense ground cover, dark red and very sweet. The air was redolent with them, and with each breeze we would push up our noses to catch the full drift. My mother hummed Edith Piaf tunes.

"It smells like a peanut butter and jelly sandwich," I reported. "Only without the peanut butter."

"We are very lucky people," she would say to me between verses. She was not unwont to cite the impoverished curbsides of Rangoon on such occasions. And when I lost interest, having collected probably five or six sandy berries along with their malicious leaves and pinched them to juice en route between ground and pot, she would gather me in her lap and tell me about her summers in East Moriches—walking among the duck farms, the raucous quacking, the choppy sea of long, tall necks in an upward-swirling cloud of white feathers; or dressing up as Romans in the backyard, with bed sheets for agora wear, and long tendrils of grape vine from the arbor that spiraled down about the head and shoulders.

I have indeed been lucky to possess both my own memories of rural pleasures and some of my mother's. What a different world that was, that entertained not only an unlicensed patch of berries but also an ungoverned welcome for the chance passerby. The next time a similar experience came my way, I was thirty years old and astounded to find wild blackberry bushes pleading for disencumberment along a roadway—but that was in South America.

You can still pick strawberries and blueberries along Route 66 west of Northampton. It won't happen on a lark on a sunny Wednesday morning, but picking hours will be conveniently advertised in the *Daily Hampshire Gazette* when the fruits are ripe. You won't be alone, but there will be plenty of branches and bushes for everyone to denude. And you can't bring a bowl from your own kitchen unless you remember to stop in the proprietor's shack and get it weighed first.

This is the famous pick-your-own concept that has seemingly revolutionized New England's small fruit and vegetable operations, giving farmers the chance to keep planting without having to pay harvest-time labor. I always thought the idea would have holes. I have watched people eat their way through apple orchards and raspberry hedges. I have seen them try none too surreptitiously to shove beets back into the ground after they have pulled up a sphere not to their liking. I have found whole stalks of corn dragged to the ground in order that someone could reach that perfect ear at the top. Even so, say some farmers, it pays. And pick-your-own farms are beloved by today's consumers, if you can judge by the growing number of farms that offer the latitude.

"People just love—they just love to root around in the dirt," said one Connecticut farmer I spoke with. "They whip up here on weekends from New York City like they're gonna see the very last red tomato ever to go ripe on God's earth. They pull up our lettuces and say, 'My God! These things have roots too. I never knew a head of lettuce had roots. Look, Sarah.'

"Ah, well, there're always a few want to know if I'm growing organic or not. I used to say no, I don't, but I'm seventy-two and I been eating my own peas for over sixty years. Now I just tell 'em where the closest organic guy is, about a half hour east of here, and I watch 'em weigh out the extra miles against their organic principles, you know. Usually they sigh, real big. And then they look at me like I put 'em in a real tight spot—a rock and a hard place—and I should feel real, real bad. And then they ask for a picking box like I should beg 'em to take what they want for nothing. Oh! the way they will stare at you. I wanta say to these folks: 'Don't forget to scrub your tomatoes real good when you get home. I gotta lotta poison on 'em.' "

But pick-your-own is not for me, not for my farm. I don't want to deal with the cars, the families, the trampled produce, and the seeming frenzy to get more than you pay for—I don't want to watch it in my fields. On that basis alone, I may be ruling out tomatoes, bulk green peas, strawberries, and other crops that are demanding to harvest, but for me it's worth it. I can find crops that are more readily manageable from the standpoint of the harvester—me. That includes: pumpkins, lettuce, zucchini, beans, herbs, cabbage, leeks, and more. If I plant for private consumption plus a little extra for family and friends, then no fruit or vegetable is out of the question. If I expand to sell to local groceries or set up a farm stand, then some varietal sacrifices may have to be made.

My husband is more interested in the horticultural side of a small farm than I am right now. He would like to raise dwarf fruit trees—pear trees, above all. If possible, he would like dense hedges of raspberry and blackberry bushes to border the property. And then, behind the house perhaps, a wildflower meadow—not too big, not too small.

"You'd better be nice to me," I have told him, "or I'll let my goats and sheep loose in your wildflower meadow." This, I thought, had to be the ultimate threat.

"I see," he said. "That's fine. Just remember to fire up the grill for all the fresh kebabs we'll be eating at dinner that night."

A standoff.

He said, "We can call your farm Parchment in a Pear Tree."

Parchment, of course, comes from animal skins.

·

"To raise crops or not to raise crops," sighed a friend. "That's a good question. Whether 'tis better to have winter vacations, or no vacations at all—the latter being the livestock scenario, by the way."

"You make a persuasive argument," I said.

"Why wouldn't you at least start out with crops?" she asked. She was wearing one of those expressions of the Terminally Reasonable.

"Whether I raise crops or animals is not a question of how to get my feet wet in farming," I said. "It's a question of whether I want to plant plants, sell plants, and plant more plants, or raise animals."

"You don't need to hunt up a veterinarian for tomatoes."

"True."

"You won't need to fight the county's nuisance laws because of unbeloved barnyard noises and smells."

"True."

"And you do not have to castrate squash."

I could see she had been saving that last remark for her finale.

"Look," I said, "I fully intend to do some cropping. We're

even looking forward to it—the draught horse I'm going to get and I."

I have a feeling that many people think that if you have success growing basil (a virtual weed) in a comely ceramic pot from Tuscany, then you can start a farming operation. There is, however, a deviation well beyond the geometric multiplication of: more basil seeds, more water, more lovely painted pots. I'll leave the issue of greenhouses and a saturated market for pesto aside for the moment. Foremost in my thinking is to convey, or remind, that all life's pleasures and hobbies are transfigured when you approach them as a business, as a livelihood. A painter, when he has to sell his canvas to buy food, will necessarily approach a subject differently than when he paints for pure enjoyment and self-exploration. People who start a nursery enterprise because they have always loved red poinsettias at Christmas will be, and abruptly so, saluted by a series of business decisions that have nothing to do with whether a poinsettia looks better on the piano or mantelpiece. It is the same for me in agriculture. The closer I come toward making my first farm purchase, the more my eyes narrow, the more I discard that wonderment-of-it-all foliage and hone in on practical economic considerations. Observing that change has been an interesting experience for me. My pleasure in the field has been completely undiminished within this evolution—in fact, I think it has grown. For one thing, it has allowed me to entertain the concept of vegetable cropping with relish, as a business, far removed from the threatening delicacies of those African violets I encounter—potted irritability flung into the house around birthday time like haphazard galactic debris from the orbit of peripheral friends.

I smiled to my friend. "I'm just scouting out a few plant varieties that will withstand my supervision. I'm waiting until the biotech companies come up with a Nora-resistant carrot. The way I see things right now, as to a verdict on crops or livestock, the question of what to raise revolves around what will best pull through the first few years of my maladroit husbandry: Bump into a cow and she may grunt, but bump into a corn stalk and it's all over. I don't like those kinds of odds. I'm clumsy by nature."

"That's why you plant a lot of everything," she said.

Crop farming as opposed to raising livestock may suit a budding farmer for several reasons. Many people are intrinsically drawn to the aesthetic of orchards, groves, and fieldrows instead of hooves, snouts, and squawks. I certainly do mean to devote a few acres to a rotation of vegetables, and perchance some cantaloupes. Already my husband and I have sat down with clean pads and pens to design clever cropping schemes and to estimate our workload and expenses. It can be a fun exercise. The analysis involved in starting a small-scale cropping enterprise is relatively straightforward. The basic cost structure of planting is logical, and one can make rough calculations for each crop year. Figure what the cost of your overhead is: land, buildings, taxes. Add together the cost of your inputs: energy, seed, labor, fertilizers, insecticides, fungicides (diatomaceous earth, lady bugs, and whale oil soap for the organic vanguard). Include the cost of your equipment: tractor, planting and harvesting and hauling attachments, maybe a computer, too. A little Total Cost addition, followed by a little Price Per Unit division (long addition but not Long Division—ask your children) goes a long way toward sketching out the general financial landscape. This is true whether it is a pound of peppers or a box of Bing cherries that you would like to sell.

Will you be selling your produce as is, or processed? I would only be selling raw agricultural produce—a bean off the vine or a pear off you-know-whose tree. But there is definitely money to be made by making forays into further processing. I know several people who don't blanche at the idea of "putting up" tomatoes and peaches for the winter. "Some of my best friends make their own jam," I am tempted to sing, lying outright to assuage the fears of the novice. In fact, for me, the prospect of processing farm yields is a notion that automatically triggers panic sirens in my brain. Suddenly all I see are federal inspectors combing my kitchen and wiretapping the dishwasher, checking that the temperature is set on Jumbo High, that no breadcrumbs lurk under my counters, that I have magnificent pension funds and workers' compensation plans for all my employees, of which there are none. Visions of blank applications and misspelled form letters flicker before my eyes. It's an incurable reflex.

Most crop farmers I have met started out with a simple recipe for growing and harvesting their produce. For many, some level of processing did arise later, the conduit usually being a wife with a knack for chutneys, pies, or breads. It's only sensible to get comfortable with your crops—the level of quality and output—before stepping into the "value-added" arena, where, to be sure, profit lies.

An attractive element of small-farm cropping is the procurement issue. Seed comes through the mail, often pretreated for diseases and common predators (prepare yourself for chalk-pink cucumber seeds). Fertilizers and pesticides are readily obtained. Rudimentary tractors and ploughs are easy to come by, or you can buy yourself a couple of handsome draught horses—but then, plainly, you're tossed back into the livestock scene. No, stay with the used tractor and keep your arithmetic simple. Then if you have a truck, a strong back, and a penchant for doing battle with cutworms, you're practically there. If you find reward in stout leafy growth and soils that may whimsically turn to brick under the summer sun—don't hesitate any longer.

Economically speaking, to survive as a small-scale vegetable farmer these days, the key seems to be (paradoxically) consistency and diversity. Supermarkets demand the former; they prefer leek bunches of identical length and nectarines of identical configuration for easy stacking. Roadside shoppers prefer the latter; they like to pitch through a crate of variously apportioned onions for The One—The Onion that calls out for nothing less than an autobiography. As a new farmer, you would do well to single out your audience, wholesale (market) or retail (consumer), and build along one of those lines. If you have huge allotments of cultivable land, you may be able to enter both markets—but then your wholesale business, where consistency of supply is next to godliness, must become a priority.

I think I would like to start cropping on a very small scale and gradually build up to modest wholesaling only when I am very comfortable with or rather proud of my yields. As a crop farmer, I know I can look forward to: bickering over cheaper supermarket prices; throwing up my hands in the face of unpredictable weather and natural predators; and coping with unsympathetic wholesale buyers as well as with organic activists, if I choose not to become one, or with furious new and unfamiliar infestations, if I decide to farm without chemicals.

That's not too bad an agenda when you compare it with animal husbandry and its own distinctive tribulations. Where do I get hay anyway? Will this truckload of corn fit happily in our garage? Why do they lamb in the middle of the night? Who's going to slaughter my hens? Can you milk my herd while I'm in Paris? What are those pink larvae around the eyes? How do I camouflage these alps of manure?

Cropping can resonate like a thoroughly benign form of farming. When you feel overwhelmed by the multitude of diverse plagues circulating through your orchard and furrows, just imagine a barnful of ailing cows and pregnant goats. When, somewhere in between the depredations of deer and woodchucks, you begin to contemplate seriously the good to be derived from nuclear arms, check yourself, and go watch a sheep farmer trying to deworm his flock. You'll feel like you made the enlightened choice.

·

There are a lot of agricultural consultants jetting around the globe these days—squarely in the business of helping farmers and politicians make all sorts of agricultural choices. I had the opportunity to meet one of them in a posh office overlooking midtown Manhattan. He had just returned from a long stretch in Eastern Europe and was finding gainful self-employment by cautioning client companies not to invest there just at the moment.

"It's a funny thing," he said, taking a deep tug on his fat cigar, "most of consulting is just common sense. I was hired by the Agriculture Ministry in Poland—or whatever the hell they're now calling their agricultural *Zentrale*—to help them solve their overwhelming farm problems. The screaming started straight-away. They said, 'By God, we are sitting under an avalanche of potatoes. Our potato processing plants are working already to capacity making frozen potatoes, french fried potatoes, mashed potatoes, canned potato soup—for Poland and half of Europe. Our storage bins are full. Our export markets are sat-urated. The prices for our farmers are dropping every year. They are worrying us with talk of strike. Every year we have such a crisis,' they said. 'What should we do?'

"What should they do?" He stubbed out his cigar. "I said to them, 'Stop planting so goddamn many potatoes!'"

Polish farmers were, of course, fighting against more than their common sense. They were confronting years of poor farm policy, Communist coercion, and repression. It takes a longer time than the observer likes to admit for a country, or for that matter a person, to change a status quo or to think fresh, outside a set of boundaries that have become curiously comfortable even if not optimal, even if not hospitable. It will take a longer time than I think many people expect for the old East and West Germany to feel *confrères* within one collective Germany. It will take a long, long time for once-Communist countries to embrace democracy in any depth.

Individuals, like nations, also become wedded to situations that may not be progressive or beneficial for them. There is a lot of comfort to be taken in the familiarity of "the old ways."

Farming probably lends itself to this tendency more than many other professions. The work is habitual, seasonal, rhythmic, manual. Change must be inserted from the outside. It doesn't sit naturally in the table of contents.

The agricultural consultant I met took full credit for turning the attentions of Polish farmers toward other crops.

"It was incredibly tough," he explained. "Farmers want to plant this spring what they planted last spring. What is it with farmers?"

However, he added, he had managed to catalyze substantial crop diversification. The apple and apple juice industries, for instance, were expanded. Had I ever tasted Polish apple juice? he asked. Well, in fact I couldn't have because it has never been exported, and, he would have to be frank with me, there is no other apple juice in the world that comes close to Polish apple juice. It is nectar.

I had heard conflicting stories about farmers as "risk takers," farmers as flexible entrepreneurs, as ready to plant carrots as kohlrabi depending upon their soil and economic incentives. In China, it seemed that as soon as the government loosened its control over agricultural production, farmers in the country-side began to produce new, higher-value crops—celery, for instance—to capture the profits allowed through greater eco-nomic freedom of choice. In Russia, however, farmers have shown themselves fundamentally less inclined to alter cropping patterns in this revolutionary new era of disassembling and re-form. There is widespread skepticism that the new free-market systems will last. And for those entrepreneurs wanting to take advantage of the freedoms offered, there is no system to assist them; machinery, distribution networks, storage facilities, even roads are in disastrous disrepair. Lack of infrastructure is one reason, I've been told, why Russia's black market gardens, those borderline-illicit quarter-hectare backyard plots that spawned flourishing economies within other once-Communist countries, seemed always beleaguered and fruitless. Another reason was Russians.

Apart from cultural *mentalité* and market access, there is another central impasse that keeps a farmer or a whole country on a rigid diet of potatoes and cabbage, years after the Potato and Cabbage for All laws have been abolished. There are long time lags and unknown risks involved in transforming one's agriculture. Moving from crops into livestock is particularly formidable, since building up a herd is expensive and can take untold years of breeding. Simply switching from one crop to another is an undertaking. Deciphering the growth cycles of new plants is a major task, the more so when you have to take into consideration each ancillary insect, disease, and nutrient need of the unfamiliar biology.

A lot of people insist that farmers are sluggish in the flexibility and modernization department, and as an ardent generalizer myself, I'm reluctant to contest the matter. The fact is, maybe that's one of the things that draws me to farming—that vast plain of unbudgeable routine, that truly bovine, unrushable pattern of sowing, shearing, feeding, breeding, cutting, drying, wintering, fallowing. In farming, there is a rigid set of limitations governing one's versatility. Farmers can't move their land to a more desirable climate. They can't manipulate the rhythms of seasons nor forfend against freaky climatic extremes. Farmers don't switch sheep breeds as a consequence of what fashions sway down the Paris runways. They can't plant extra acres in corn so as to afford the new "must-have" Range Rover. They don't get paid extra for working late, and they call their own shots on sick days.

Friends of mine who have become eminently successful within the financial swirls of Wall Street are often the first to say they wish they could do what I am doing. They will sigh, feet on the desk, thumbs under the suspenders, eyes on the city traffic forty storeys below. They seem tired of having to keep up with society's glamorous, endless spewing of new trends. Tired but not released. Ah well, urbanity is a little addictive. I have watched these friends mark the seasons with changes of clothes and home decor. They adjust themselves continually and intemperately to keep up with modern times. They complain of being over-worked, constantly in demand. To relax, they mass in obscure seaside spas and have their eyelashes dyed. They rail about the fatuousness of other people's conversation, the emptiness of other people's lives. And then they file into therapy, one by one, to find out why they themselves feel so empty in spite of their pots of gold.

Perhaps I, too, will feel empty after years of farming. After all, farming is not *more* of a way of life compared to other professions. It's just different. I wonder often what will become of me as a farmer. I hope it isn't unrealistic to think about reading in the evenings, or writing. Limberness can gel. Will I become one of those inflexible, tied-to-her-eggplants farmers? Spinster-like qualities can creep into lives of unmitigated routine and worry. Will I make myself a relic after years of struggling to participate in society? Resenting the luxuries of other lives must have to be a possibility. I wonder. Will I long for a more monied lifestyle?

No. I don't think so. First of all, I have always found the status quo unsettling. It's not my strongest point, and I have a history of seeking out a steady daily routine and then deftly toppling it; but perhaps that will protect me from premature hardening of the brain synapses. Second, I could never become a recluse. Who would I talk to if I were a recluse? And third, I don't find today's wealth so glamorous or seductive. It seems to be concentrated in the hands of the classless. The affluent appear to me to be an unreflective, extravagant, and intellectually hollow lot. Just think about Nancy Reagan. Just look at the Trump clan. No thank you. The data is there. Money must surely pervert one. Besides, I never wanted a yacht.

"Although," said one of my sisters, "I think you might have been perfectly radiant as a rich and warring Medici."

It was true.

•

One summer I helped Cal, a farmer in Connecticut, plant his annual agenda of vegetables. Cal's foreman had disappeared suddenly after a drunken driving accident and left Cal short-handed in the middle of sowing season. When I joined him, he was preparing to transplant his tomatoes. He had grown three varieties of tomato in his greenhouses in the valley—Celebrity, Early Girl, and Beefsteak. By early June the seedlings were be-tween eight and twelve inches tall in their little peat pots, and it was time to move them out. The ground was warm enough. Tomatoes love warmth. "Summertime, and the fruiting is easy," they hum. But by June it gets so hot in a greenhouse that even tomatoes can feel a little sluggish, lose their stiff, upright pos-tures, and complain illustratively of suffocation.

The tomatoes had been started in peat pots arranged in flats, the ubiquitous plastic trays that nurserymen use to hold sets of flowers and lettuces and so forth for retail customers. They are maddening things. Nothing could be better suited to standard-ization than those flat, low-lipped, rectangular plastic trays for holding sets of smaller plastic boxes of seedlings for transplant. But are they? No. Every inspired American plastic tray manu-facturer wants to put his signature on the design. As a conse-quence, after every growing season gardeners and nurserymen alike wake up to topographical knolls on their property com-posed of hundreds of slightly uncomforming—flexible and non-flexible, grooved and nongrooved, this one too squared, that one too shallow—perfectly unstackable black, green, and gray flats. Simple in design, they seduce you with images of lavish practicality. It's hard to throw them out, although since they don't stack or fold they tend to take up inordinate amounts of storage space. They are uglier than powerboats when they sit in your driveway (they're even more abhorrent in your neighbor's driveway), poking up through the first snow, feebly suggesting a higher purpose, nonbiodegradable and finally begging to be delivered to the hazardous waste dump. Plastic garden flats will outlive us all.

The tomatoes I was to transplant for Cal sat in their hothouse flats in varied arrangements. They were growing in peat pots, which also defy sensible uniformity and turn up round and square, two by two inches or three by three, stiff or crumbly. The whole dirt floor of the greenhouse was covered in these rich green tomato seedlings, densely aligned and pungent in the humid interior air. When these were gone, the greenhouse flaps would be taped open to let breezes through, and the dirt floor would be given over to portulaca and dahlia cultivation.

Cal had already ploughed furrows up at the farm and laid down a sprinkling of fertilizers. Early on a Thursday morning, we loaded his ramshackle old truck with hundreds of tomato flats and headed, literally, for the hills. The farm unfolded on the crest of a Berkshire foothill. It was divided into irregular plots by unruly hedgerows and tractor paths. Altogether there were eighty acres available for sowing. It was cropped normally in sweet corn, beets, peas, peppers, tomatoes, lettuces, spinach, strawberries, and cauliflower, but because of poor weather conditions that spring, only half of the total acreage was suitable for planting, and only in tomatoes, peppers, and a smattering of corn. Drought was forecast throughout New England that summer, and Cal had no irrigation systems set up to compensate. Farmers in that area had traditionally relied on natural rainfall.

It was hot and dry the day we hopped off the truck. We were: two illegal farm workers from Puerto Rico, Sammy and Honario, together with their coolers full of whiskey, cigarettes, and packaged bologna; Maria, a round seventy-year-old Polish woman who had lived successfully in the States for forty years without once learning a single word of English; myself in shorts, work boots, and sunglasses engineered to protect one from the worst of alpine ultraviolet rays; and Cal, the boss, who stood inside the shade of the rickety truck and handed flats of tomatoes to us one after another. We made quite a crew. Sammy and Honario chatted constantly in rapid-fire Spanish about their brothers and cousins back in Puerto Rico. Maria sang unknown, uncomposed songs to herself. She had a habit of giggling wildly when someone said her name, a reflex that the Puerto Ricans noticed and which they periodically exploited as a distracting game. Cal smoked, inventoried, and remained quiet.

I was going gangbusters for the first couple of hours, skipping across the furrows with my heavy (just watered) tomato flats, bending, straightening, bending, straightening, dropping individual plants onto the pink and white fertilizer crystals in the rows. We took a break at ten for a Coke, which was a mistake since sodas make you thirsty. And from there it just got bad. The sun was rising higher. A breeze cropped up. It whisked the dry silts of one ploughed field into another. Silt can be like talc against your skin, soaking up the perspiration and then sticking around, coating you. The tomato seedlings must have felt the same way—parched by the sun, pushed by the breezes, and finally shrouded in a fine, powdery soil. What a shower wouldn't do for me, they affirmed in unison, picturesquely drooping as proof.

My sunglasses were falling constantly off my face and into the soil. They would slip forward slightly from the perspiration, and then plunge down the cliff of my Roman nose—a genetic liability for glasses-wearing people in the most unoffending of climates. By eleven o'clock my boots felt like a pair of thirty-pound barbells. I couldn't seem to lift my feet high enough to clear a furrow ridge. Smack, smack, smack, I went along, kicking more dry silts into the air and gradually destroying the aesthetic of Cal's evenly ploughed rows. I felt like one of Rommel's soldiers in the middle of the Serengeti, dying of thirst before the enemy even got close.

"Rommel was on the wrong side," said my husband. "First. And second, he wasn't in the Serengeti, he was in North Africa."

I was stepping out of a Siamese hot box along the River Kwai, thrusting each deadened foot forward after days of starvation and intense tropical heat, proud in front of my soldiers, mum to the enemy interrogators.

My back ached and the backs of my legs were throbbing. I glanced over at Maria, fresh and patient, forcing open the knotted roots of each plant before dropping them into the furrows. She was singing the same entropic assortment of notes. I saw Sammy and Honario, quieter now under the almost rhythmic pulse of sun, but smoking, lithe.

Kalahari, I was saying to myself. Kalahari. Water. Hey, Cal, did you bring any water?

No, but I got a Coke here with your name on it.

Show me a hospital cot with my name on it.

Ultimately, I made it through the day, but I looked like I hadn't.

"Do you have to go back tomorrow?" asked my husband. He was worried. "You look awful."

"Thanks," I said. "I haven't had enough exposure to peasant farming yet. But tomorrow we have to put the stakes in for these tomatoes and Cal needs to fix some of the fencing that rings the vegetable fields. He's having deer problems. I said I'd be there."

The work became easier each day. My energy improved. My endurance grew. My muscles tightened. Farming seemed to pull each part of me in alternation—the backs of my arms, my wrists, my calves, my stomach, my thighs. Every sinew was suddenly gainfully employed. The drought continued, but I was thriving.

We staked the tomatoes, harvested the lucky spring peas and strawberries, planted green peppers that we knew wouldn't survive the heat and dryness. Cal had a friend that filled people's swimming pools with fresh water from his truck. Once in a while, when he was free from the demands of pool owners—

usually at around nine at night—he would come by the farm and spray water over the fields. It made little impact on the wilting plants.

Then came the deer, the woodchucks, squirrels, possum, and raccoons, creatures likewise suffering under the drought and deprived of their usual food supplies. They seemed to be gathering in greater and greater numbers in Cal's fields, eating by night the few plants that we managed to keep alive through the day.

"I may lose this crop year to God," said a miserable Cal one morning. "But I sure as hell am not going to lose it to a pack of four-legged forest-rats." That's what he called deer.

So Cal upped the charge on his electric fence, strung a strand of barbed wire along the top of his wooden fence, and brought a sleeping bag out to the farm shed to keep guard in person.

"*Loco*," said Sammy, gesturing toward Cal. Sammy and Honario were these days busier clearing deer carcasses from the perimeters of the fields than cultivating crops. There was little work for me, but I would drive by now and then to check in on Cal. The fields had turned to dust. I would find Cal sometimes oiling and cleaning his tractor, sometimes oiling and cleaning his rifle. Drought clobbered farmers throughout New England that year. Cal sold off a piece of his hilltop farmland to a developer. The following year the weather was favorable and he had a bumper crop on his seventy-seven and a half acres.

Farming.

You have to expect with cropping that a lot of fauna in this world will be as excited about your plants as you are. Predators for your wheat crop may be locusts, for your tomatoes may be beetles, for your cabbages may be worms, for your celery may be deer. The deer that daily take their salads among our beans and tulip petals—your garden-variety deer—are growing rapidly in numbers throughout sections of America. Restrictions on hunting have allowed regional populations to flourish, butting up against our own (human beings') intensive urban and suburban population growth. They are ingesting beloved shrubs, pulverizing the windshields of expensive European cars, and so arousing fewer whimpers as their outstretched carcasses lie in larger numbers along the breakdown lanes of not so country roads.

Many crop farmers will keep old rifles around for scaring deer off, if not for liquidating one or two. A farmer I know in Fairfield keeps something like a vintage blunderbuss well cleaned and oiled in his field shed. He is seventy-two and nearly blind, and people who know about the gun find the whole image rather disconcerting.

"The only thing I hate more'n deers is deer lovers," he once growled to me.

I knew another farmer in Massachusetts who sustained a similar hatred for moles. His zucchini and lettuce fields were a bas relief maze of holes and ridges sculpted by dint of a zealous population of these burrowers. Although he had been farming organically for years, he finally gave it up so that he could gas the tunnels. He used a rifle, too.

"Maybe they'll start selling twenty-two-gauge shotguns next to the hoes at Agway," I said to my husband.

He said, "Target practice will become a mandatory class at all the agricultural schools."

•

When we lived in Connecticut, the garden was my husband's greatest spring pleasure. He, who had never been a notable early bird, would be up at six in the morning on weekdays to fit in a little hoeing or planting before going to work. The amount of tending that this garden demanded would fluctuate radically from day to day.

"Oh dear. It says we have got to put the spinach in today at the latest," my husband would grumble, leafing through his manuals.

"I see here that the last frost for our area is April one," he would report.

"We absolutely can't put the lettuce where it was last year," came his fiat.

The garden demanded a lot of work, alongside his job. Occasionally he would, with the proper amount of fear in his voice, ask for my help. It usually meant weeding or reseeding somewhere.

"Where exactly?" I would ask (thunder).

Around the calendula, in between the tomatoes and the cabbage, at the end of the cucumber circles.

"Cucumber circles?" I smiled.

"You'll see them at the end of the rows, close to the woodchuck hole—I've planted them in little craters, in a circle."

"Are you sure I'll know a cucumber sprout from a weed?"

"Oh yes," he would say. "Cucumbers have two fat round leaves. They look . . . attractive. And there will be three in each crater. Whereas the weeds will be everything else. Actually," he sighed, "the weeds will probably look more robust."

"I really don't want to take chances with your cucumbers," I said. It was true. I don't like being set up for an unintentional kill.

"Don't worry," said my husband, "you can't miss them."

"Okay," I would whistle, tying up the laces of my steel-toed work boots, slipping my hands into farrier's gloves, and ambling out to the garage to select some monster tool with which, I imagined, in two broad strokes I could make child's play of this weeding marathon. "Noooo problem."

"I really appreciate your help," my husband would say, obviously hesitant to leave.

So out I went to the garden, a few things like saws, awls, and vine cutters over my shoulder, and I set to work. One glance toward the cucumber craters and I decided to leave them until last. The craters were thick with weeds and stinging nettles. A lot of things seemed "fat" and a few even seemed attractive. There were little purple and white blossoms everywhere. I would kick off my search-and-save mission in a bit, I decided, once I had had some practice with the more defined lettuce rows. Maybe I would have to buy my husband a tractor—get away from this Lilliputian nightmare.

Inevitably, it seemed, when my troubled head made one of its rare appearances among the harrowed rows, our over-the-hedge neighbor would find me and hail me. She was a beautiful Cuban woman married to the president of a huge mining corporation, and she was president herself of a local garden club. She was often to be found out on their broad lawn, pruning bushes and cutting fresh bouquets for their house. When she would see me in the garden, she would trot over smiling. She looked at me with an evangelist's eyes.

Then, "Deer!" she nearly spat that morning. This kind of vehemence was highly unlike her.

"Are they troubling you?" I asked. In the back of my mind I wondered whether our well-fed woodchuck wasn't actually at the root of her rancor.

"Don't you see?" she screamed—in a friendly way. "Hoof-prints everywhere. Why, they have been holding conferences and board meetings in my impatiens bed. You really must now put fences around your garden. High, high fences. After all your work, I would hate them to eat your vegetables. Oh and look!" She cast a glance toward the ground. "Your cucumbers are doing so marvelously!"

I dropped my saws and ran over to her.

"Where?"

8

Sacred Cows

"Who doesn't love a cow?" said a friend of mine.

I gave the question some thought. It has been my experience that the only people who don't coo about cows are ranchers. Talk to ranchers. Some of them just can't stand cattle. "So stupid," they will grimace. "So so so stupid." And this considered opinion comes from years of involvement—gathering herds from the range, running them through chutes, testing them for pregnancy, impregnating those that require it, finding lost calves on the range, regathering herds for shipping, loading frightened steers onto trucks, and so on. All of this might be less cumbersome if cattle were brighter, is the cowboy's theory. Brighter, but not brighter than cowboys.

My first introduction to ranching came with a semester off from college in 1980. I took the opportunity to work for a beef cattle company in Casper, Wyoming, where a friend of my sister had also once been hired. The owners of the ranch, the Lazy X, were brothers. They had taken over an old sheep operation and converted it to handle about sixteen hundred head of Angus and Hereford cattle. The conversion had been simple. It necessitated some fence repairs, fresh barn supports, and the dislodging of several layers of sedimentary sheep manure from some of the paddocks. The brothers had borrowed a huge Caterpillar backhoe to accomplish the last task, so compacted were the years of manure; within the layers they had found old shearing tools and whiskey bottles.

"Nope, farming hasn't changed much at all," one of the brothers had remarked, referring to all the liquor bottles he had excavated.

When I first arrived at the Lazy X, many of the old tools and bottles had been hung, unwashed and still encrusted, for decoration in the bunkhouse. I thought, after some months at the ranch, that these filthy relics were a good illustration of the ambient aesthetic and the parsimonious nature of the brothers. It was a neglected place. It conveyed the near impossibility of restoration without first committing to demolition.

I spent most of my first weeks inside the dilapidated barns, checking one pen of heifers (first-time mothers) for pregnancy, helping another set calve. There were birthing problems every day. Calves got twisted in the umbilical cord, or had turned themselves around backward, or would hook a shoulder or hoof on the way out. In these instances the farmhands had to help with delivery to keep the calf from being severely injured. "Helping" started with tying down the frantic and bellowing mother cow, since she didn't think she needed help. There is a trick to this, the crooking back of one front leg, and then if necessary, the disarmament of a defensive rear leg. Someone explained to me that cows need both front legs to get up, so if you can get a purchase on one . . . Of course, that leaves wide open the issue of getting them down on their sides to begin with, and on this Casper ranch, depending on what time of night everyone had been roused, that sometimes translated into an intemperate kicking of the cow and belting her with a two-by-four block of wood. At the time I found no justification for this behavior from the ranch's foreman and owners, and I cannot now.

Oddly enough, in spite of the violence with which some of those calves came into the oxygenated world, the births still gave me that precious sensation of miracle. One calf would gush out in a river of blood and placenta, shiny wet, pitch black, blinking, face first into the golden straw. We would set it up near its exhausted mother and she would begin to lick the tissue from its shaking body. I would bottle-feed colostrum to the sick, weak-legged, or rejected calves, and I thought that there was nothing in the world so wonderful as the warm and butting head of a seeking, hungry calf. I still think there is little that is *more* wonderful.

I reflect with a sense of gratitude on my months at this crude ranch. My love of the work and of the place itself surpassed my dislike of the management. I was forever captivated by the seasonal changes in that unfamiliar landscape. Casper offered striking vistas, markedly lunar in one direction, Mediterranean in another. The ranch was situated in a kind of vast, flat basin that allowed the uninterrupted furor of periodic storms to gather momentum as they swept across the broad skies. The weather was never gentle, the winds were unmitigated, and the ground seemed as hardened as the bleached, bleak skulls of antelope that littered it.

"Be prepared for blizzards through June," they had cautioned me. Indeed, it was toward the end of May when a stunning force of snow whipped through the Casper basin and buried cattle and vehicles under ten-foot drifts in a matter of hours. We had gone out on horseback to drive whatever cattle we could find from the draws—the nearly crevasslike cleavages of eroded earth that seemed to drop everywhere, out of nowhere, throughout the spread of the ranch. The snow was swirling so densely and shrilly around us that we often lost our bearings. At times we were literally blinded. We couldn't hear one another over the winds, and we relied on occasional glimpses of horse and rider to ascertain the strategy, success, or despair of the other hands. Then, as quickly as the storm had come, it was gone. And the earth was not savage, but crystalline and beautiful and somehow innocent as the snow dripped and melted and formed rills that carved deeper against those same sheer draws.

We lost some cows and calves in that storm, and they were frightening to find—rigid with cold and rigor mortis in contorted positions of frantic flight. We sequestered the carcasses in a remote gully, making a rubble heap of mangy hides pronged with taut dead legs and hooves. It became a grand feast for the coyotes, wolves, buzzards and prairie dogs that lived in the forsaken reaches of the ranch.

Come late spring, the earth was transformed into a knee-deep mire of slick mud. Day after day, tractors would get stuck in the wet clay as they tried to pull other, already embedded trucks and tractors out of it. Sometimes work would wait upon twenty-four hours of gray skies and rainless wind until we could finally drive the fleet of sunken, mud-encumbered vehicles out of the slowly solidifying ground. No one cursed the rains, because the ranch's alfalfa cultivation depended upon every drop that could be garnered, stored, channeled, or absorbed before summertime.

By July, the rainfall ceased. The air cleared of storm clouds, a dry wind blew, and all the ranchers in the area would drive out to inspect their irrigation dikes and clear the ditches of tumbleweeds. In the Western states, landowners rely on their privately owned water rights to obtain a continuous flow or trickle of fresh water throughout the dry summer months. The Lazy X was fortunate to hold first water rights to Barretts Creek, an unimpressive but vital flow of water that wound through the Casper basin. This last bit of water gave the ranch a significant edge on local alfalfa hay production, and it allowed us to graze animals further into the arid season before driving them onto higher ground.

The dry-weather season would arrive as quickly as those freakish spring blizzards. It immediately parched the ground, which had been ripped up into violent seas during the wet season, and which now hardened overnight into sharp peaks and pitted ruts that punctured our vehicles' tires and injured animals each day.

"It's pure adobe," said the foreman to me as he kicked brick-hard spikes of earth from sections of the farmyard. "Straw, water, and clay."

The ranch gradually whitened over the summer—a kiln-fired white. My morning chores kept me around the barns, where I could look out, from a slight rise in the earth, onto miles of parched land peppered by the black dots of distant Angus cattle foraging for the spare bits of grass, or the gray green of sagebrush and the aimless, atomic circling of tumbleweeds.

This is the land that steaks come from, I mused—not the fancy, corn-fed, perfectly marbled steaks of Omaha reputation, but a volume of tougher, leaner steaks (in an era when lean was not so preferred), chuck roasts, and hamburger that sustained a large portion of our nation and populations across the world. At that ranch, we also ate our own meat, fresh meat only hours old. It came not from young steers that we herded across the gullies, but from old cows that were no longer reproducing.

"Them's the Eat-ums," explained the foreman to me as we pitched hay into a pen of about eight five-year-old Angus cows. I had thought at first he said "Edam," meaning that these were a novel breed of cattle from Holland. Fortunately, I asked no betraying follow-up questions, and later on during my stay there I was informed in clear terms about their fate. Sure enough, as the months passed, the population in the pen diminished. A local man came by the ranch every six weeks or so to shoot and butcher one of them. He would hang two hot sides of beef in our cooler, where they were left to bleed down and "cure." I thought the eat-um meat tasted awful, fresh or frozen, but I suspect this had to do as much with my aversion to slaughter at the time as anything else.

"I only like the first half of husbandry," I wrote home to my mother. "The raising half."

•

The lifestyle of a livestock farmer is a frequent subject for consideration. One has to enjoy the daily chores, since one faces them 365 days of the year. My husband and I have had to come to grips with the fact that neither beef cattle nor dairy cattle take holidays. Beef cattle may, under profoundly desirable circumstances, offer up periods of virtual self-sufficiency, in that they can pasture fairly well. That is, they may be left to graze for weeks in open grasslands with a trifling amount of consultation. On a working ranch, cowboys will set out salt licks, molasses blocks, or supplemental feeds, but the actual tending of the cattle could be light. During these stretches, fences are repaired, barns built, grains or grasses cultivated, and feedlots contracted. It's actually a busy time for cattlemen, a time to catch up on long-neglected problems. And for the small stock farmer lucky enough to have a rambling range of a backyard, this may be a pleasantly quiet time of the year or breeding cycle. It is, unfortunately, not the perfect interval to jet to Bermuda unless you have hired someone else to look, now and again, over all those bovine shoulders for a sign of imperfect behavior—someone who knows what to do with stampeded fences, very pregnant cows, sick cows, or cows that have wandered into an alfalfa field and pretty well exploded.

With dairy cows, business is particularly ruthless in its effect on vacation plans. Dairying demands your full attention, every day of the year—once, twice, or even three times a day. When you have one cow, you can manage this by hand. I am told that beyond five cows, hand-milking is akin to self-flagellation with no sublime laurels on the other end. What happens to many farmers is that they purchase a milking machine for their ten cows or so, but then the milking goes by so quickly that they decide to buy a few more cows. Sound economics—and it helps to amortize that infernal machine. So, with a herd of twenty or thirty cows, the day seems full. But maybe a little too full, since each time a farmer finishes milking he must assiduously clean all the machinery. Dairy parlors are hotbeds of bacterial achievement and are therefore well monitored by state and federal inspectors—so sterilizing equipment becomes a significant portion of a dairyman's day. Not only can you find yourself desperate for a vacation, but you will wonder how it is you got into the agricultural machinery and sanitation business.

With dairying, I think it is particularly important to deliberate over the issue of scale. The difference between managing five cows and twenty is not geometric, but exponential. In the first instance you have taken on a chore that brings you fresh warm milk and some sort of satisfaction. In the second instance you have taken on a business that involves cattle, cattle breeding, machinery, a parlor complete with stalls, and, hopefully a competent cooperative milk pool with its own hauling system somewhere in the county.

I'm reminded of a college friend who started a brewery in Boston. He told me that when his company was small he was able to concentrate full time on his beer recipe. As the company grew larger, he felt he had become manager of a bottle cleaning and recycling operation, with beer production as a trivial sideline. I heard a parallel story from an innkeeper who expanded his Vermont lodge. In retrospect, he said, he had quit the inn business and found himself in the linen-laundering business. I think that with dairying you run something of the same risk. The labor demands shift with size, as does the amount of time you spend in front of a computer, as does the equipment you will be required to purchase. Once you subscribe to any significant scale of operation, you had better bone up on your sciences. You will need to know which detergents are safe, what temperatures are best, how suction milkers can be most efficiently managed, and what iodine dips can and cannot prevent.

I keep this in mind always as I plan for a small farm. Small it will start, and small in many ways I expect it will stay. My objective is not to gain some scale whereby I can hire extra help and buy heavy machinery—it is to do the farming myself, to enjoy the farming itself. I happen to love the work. I have to love the work, I believe, because a farmer's day-to-day options for reneging are few and his struggles are legion.

You have to have a clear objective before you get into the cattle business. There will always be that person whose daddy was a rancher, and his daddy, and his daddy's daddy . . . but if you are going to take up the saddle or the milk pail with no ancestral inclinations to speak of, then I believe you need to want something at the other end. Badly. I guarantee you will need a strong scaffolding of purpose to hang on to on the lousy days.

Possible pitfalls need mentioning, if only briefly. Otherwise they might come on you fast and furious, and you would feel inundated with irreconcilable problems, guilty feelings, maybe even frostbite or a strained back. You might thrust about looking for someone to sue under the Agricultural Hard Truths in Advertising Act, and in a burst of frustration, you might even decide to sue me under the Misleading Fun on the Farm Publications Clause. But if you feel adequately warned about those black flies and humid days, you can skip the next few paragraphs and never bemoan them.

Whether you decide to raise beef or dairy cattle, there are times when trials seem to arrive by the busload. Your feed supplier turns unreliable in the middle of winter. An unusual virus seems to be sweeping through your barn. Two weeks of deluging spring rains have made a marsh of your pasture, rotted your haystacks, and weakened your calves. And here in the middle of summer, black flies have made your air opaque. I don't like to enumerate these hapless scenarios, least of all to myself, but if you come upon them without warning you might feel singularly hapless—as I have at times. Working cattle just has its days. I keep alive for myself some nettling memories of cattle husbandry in order to stay honest and candid about my own expectations.

Consider those moments, I reflect, of trying to move cattle. Only man bests cattle when it comes to preferring the status quo. But when you weigh nine hundred pounds and you have no inclination to head to higher pastures, the wealth of prerogative would seem to be on your side. Pity the poor cowhand who rises at three thirty in the morning to begin the cattle drive to summer ranges. It is still pitch black as you ride your horse out onto the range. Gradually your eyes grow accustomed to the dark. Valleys and hillsides sprinkled with the stationary black figures of sleeping cattle grow clearer. Cattle drives traditionally commence this early, removed from the heat of noon, and calmly, so as not to spook the animals. You gather the cattle on horseback and gently nudge them along a path they know—cattle remember the trails surprisingly well from year to year. Without much fuss, calves to their mothers' hocks, they file along. This makes for a homey picture until something a little out of the ordinary comes up—you have to cross a roadway, there is a steep incline, the head cattle are startled by a coyote, or you have just pushed too far at one time. Uh-oh.

Suddenly an active yeast of dissension seems to be fermenting in this river of black hides. The usual cacophony of intermittent bellows and *maaaaas* (the calves looking for their familiar udders) is working its way indisputably into a crescendo. From behind the herd, you watch the surface energy of black backs grow turbulent. The momentum is no longer forward. Shoulder is butting against shoulder. There is a bottleneck up front for some reason, a refusal to dare forward. Black heads shove their wet noses above the black horizon as they get squeezed from back and front. A whitecap of cattle froth is caught by the wind and sent drifting through the air. The diarrhea starts.

They are agitating up front in an old irrigation ditch along the side of the highway, which must be crossed. The fence is open. There is no traffic. But the ditch sides are perhaps a little sheer for these exquisite hooves. And then, before you can do anything else (or your partner either, and you should have one), the dam breaks and black hides swim backward beside you, not in stampede but with the assured gusto of a declined invitation. You are only lucky this didn't happen on the road itself, on the slippery (to hooves) asphalt, with a line of uranium miners in their Dodge trucks heading to work the five a.m. shift while a seeming gusher of black bodies—those not splayed across the tarmac—spill into the grassy channels between road and barbed-wire fence in a frightened frenzy.

You think, I only need one bullet.

There is another cattle-related incident I recollect on a small New England feedlot where I once worked. A large black Saler steer, unhinged after weeks of rain, escaped onto the concrete walkways between the cattle pens. He had bounded over the railing, which should be a reminder to aspiring cattlemen that their wards are actually adept at leaping. Finding himself all alone on the wet and manure-slick concrete, this steer panicked. He charged off in one direction that incidentally led to the feedlot's big manure pit, which, after those weeks of rain, was in a disagreeable state of foment. The steer, taking his bearings on the run and suddenly spotting this soupy brown pond, put on his brakes. Four wet steaming hooves ground to a halt—but not the steer. He had been running too fast to let the mere suspension of his stride interrupt his progress. Those four en-chanting hooves danced, skidded stylishly past the last pen, past two unbelieving feedlot employees, past the hay bales, and then painfully down down down the slippery ramp into the manure pit, with what can only be called a "slurp."

The steer survived. He was eventually roped and hauled out of the wet manure by five stunned and recoiling men. I had never seen a steer look miserable before—much less humiliated.

I remember, too, helping out one winter day with a pregnancy testing program on a Wyoming Hereford ranch. It was way below zero that morning, and dark. We were stationed in a small barn where a long and sinuous cattle chute led in from outside and wound to a halt, its iron-levered "squeeze cage" before us. The squeeze cage was basically in the form of a V, which clapped tight and reopened to hold and then release an animal within. Cows and heifers from a corral behind the barn were being fed gradually into the chute. Each would be retained in the iron cage while checked for pregnancy; then the cage would be opened and the cattle let loose into another corral in front of the barn.

Cattle don't like to be separated from the herd. They like even less being prodded into narrow passageways, to the hooted urgings of cowhands, along a dark and unfamiliar path toward dim lights ahead. It was clearly a gross ordeal for these two- and three-year olds as they bellowed through the chute, their eyes bulging open to show white and rolling unnervingly backward. Every now and then one tried to turn herself around and got inextricably wedged—nine hundred pounds of muscle forcibly thrusting itself into a knot in the middle of a thin steel corridor—halfway down, while another frightened and snorting heifer was careening down the chute only feet behind her.

"Imagine a snake," I said to my husband, "with one elephant caught in its throat and another just swallowed whole."

As each animal barreled down the chute toward the squeeze cage, one of the gathering cowhands would warn us with a "Heifer!" or "Cow!" Standing by the open squeeze cage, another man waited until the animal's whole body was clean within the confines of the frame. Then he would yank the lever down slamming two iron panels up against her flanks. A leather brace clapped the cow's neck and left her pretty well immobilized, bawling, hooves often off the ground. The impact of the squeeze chute could be extremely powerful.

"So," I had smiled to the cowhand at the squeeze cage, "ever break any ribs?"

"Dunno, lady," he muttered.

His was not the preferred job. It is a fast rule of these operations that the chute cage becomes coated with the runny manure from one apprehensive cow after another. Cattle are quick to flush their loose bowels in a moment of alarm, so the walls of the entire squeeze chute were promptly caked and steaming with hot manure. Few of us escaped the morning unbedecked.

My job as I stood freezing in that barn was to check off the identification numbers from each animal's ear tag and make a note of whether she was pregnant or not. Those not pregnant were administered a hormone shot to start them on their heat cycle again. I jotted down the date so that the hands would know when later to re-inseminate.

By ten in the morning I had lost feeling in both my feet and was stomping across the straw-covered wood boards to revive any sensation. Our only heat was emanating from two bare bulbs that hung, one above a small table full of charts, hypodermic needles, and assorted medicinal vials, the other above the terminus of the squeeze chute where a local vet was repeatedly plunging his arm into the rectum of each Hereford female to check her ovaries. He wore a long manila rubber glove, which he hosed off from time to time with what must have been nearly freezing water.

"Gotsta hopes," he grinned at me once, his arm lost inside a heifer, "she gets the runs on the ways ins. I hates when they gets their die-harreas bys me here in the squeeze."

•

I do have dreams to carry me through the less attractive hours of cattle tending. There are two, in fact, that I have been nursing along with respect to my small farm. The first answers a fundamental question of purpose, the second responds to something even deeper.

The first dream (which, as I get closer to owning my farm, must assume the stature of a tangible objective) is to breed rare and old races of animals—to create a kind of livestock seedbank. I have heard of people doing this on a small scale, raising some peculiar breeds of poultry and cattle that had no coveted market traits and so have been gradually forsaken by commercial farmers. I, too, would like to raise and protect the old breeds. I think mankind has been prodigal with its agricultural resources, both plant and animal, too short-sighted in its self-appointed gov-

ernment of species and too willing to jettison entire breeds
before we can even be sure what they can offer. Species extinction, oddly enough, doesn't seem to quicken a lot of pulses. I
suspect that's because its consequences cannot be quantified or
adequately envisioned. We occasionally hear about a smallish
monkey or a largish bird on the verge of vanishing completely—only five dispirited specimens between that species'
continuance and another color illustration in the history books.
They tend to be in countries we never visit, in puddles we never
look into. They tend to resemble every other monkey or blackish
bird that we have had the luck to see. If there were so few
anyway, we mull, maybe they were just gradually dying out in
proper Darwinian fashion. A kind of owl in Vermont. A kind
of minnow in Utah. Look, we add, we can't spend millions
resuscitating an owl when we have so many social problems to
address.

In agriculture, many breeds of animals have been neglected
or even crossbred out of existence in attempts by man to beget
specific traits. This worries a lot of people who think that if your
genetic base is too thin you risk an unknown scourge—a virus
or cancer, for example—that could wipe out an entire animal
population. Others suggest that, with climatological changes
such as are proposed by the greenhouse effect, our entire agriculture will change, and the few breeds we currently rely upon
will become impractical overnight. It's not difficult to discern
the tinges of extremism here—but I do agree that we human
beings have lost an appreciation for the variation that used to
abound. We are forsaking the broad and fabulous reverberations
of hybrid vigor, and supplanting them with precise methods of
gene trading.

"Ridiculous!" said a cattle breeder to me. "There's still plenty
of hybrid vigor among today's breeds. Do you know how long
a strand of DNA is? My god, that's just feet and inches full of
variation."

Yes and no, I think. There are a lot of minuscule variations among computers, too. The fact is that most of the dairy cows in America belong to one of two breeds, and I have heard that eighty percent of these cows are artificially inseminated by a semen pool collected from around twenty bulls, most likely all of whom are now deceased. Variation? It's moot.

I think we will discover very late in the game why genetic diversity among livestock is still critical, and how some of the bygone breeds might have imparted worthwhile traits.

"My farm will teem with unmarketable breeds," I said to a friend one day. "The too-small cattle, the ones that don't give enough milk, the ones best suited to draught work, which is nobody's interest in this industrial world."

"You don't shock me," said my friend. "I was sitting next to you when you tried to flunk economics at Harvard. Still, if you could find a breed that didn't moo too loudly or that produced only prime steaks, then you might have something valuable to sell."

My farm may be a repository of information about the older races, and I could be a source to both biologists and breeders. My notes will be tight, my observations useful to the cattleman. And would there be a market for the semen from these bygone breeds? I have wondered whether modern breeders would find any interest in crossing their fine, towering dams with my curious stock. I have a sense there would be some interest. After all, breeders are constantly having to modify their lines to gratify changing consumer tastes—making the average entrecote smaller or larger, for example, to suit the current household size—or to suit different geographical markets. There is also the chance that environmental flux and environmentalist fervor may force livestock producers to rethink their practices and their "ideal" animals. In times of transition there is always a renewed interest in fresh input. In the livestock business, that means fresh genetic material. Maybe, if I were to keep such a storehouse, I wouldn't have to lose so much money after all.

"Can we use conventional barns for these ancient breeds?"

my husband asked with humor. "No dinosaurs in the dell or anything?"

"No dinosaurs," I said. "Actually, most of the unfashionable breeds are small beast material. Good for parties. Won't threaten the neighbors. Dishwasher safe."

"I've got a great idea," he laughed. "We could open up a restaurant. I'd man the grill, of course. We'd serve only steaks from old, old breeds of cattle. Tuesday could be Neanderthal Night. It's getting clearer now. And down the road, ice cream from the milk of some ancient race of cows . . ."

I said, "I get your meaning. But it sounds a little macabre, no?"

He said, "We can call your farm Nora's Ark."

I was content enough with the aim of raising the older breeds on my farm. But there is another dream I have been nursing along and that I still hope to braid into my cattle operation. I want to make my farm accessible to physically and emotionally handicapped children. I want to give these children the chance to put their own foreheads against the hot flank of a milking cow, to poke their fingers down an amazing four inches into the greasy wool of a ewe. Tending livestock, in my own life, tapped into a profound internal well. It gave me a unique and precious province which was my first real autonomy from the broad-reaching specialties of my siblings and parents. It also broke into a long-standing loneliness that had begun to enfold me at ten, when my mother became ill, and had gradually wrapped its strangling self in layers around me by the time she died, eleven years later. Handling livestock turned this loneliness into a hospitable aloneness. I have dreamt ever since of providing a similar opportunity to troubled children—not anticipating a remedy for them, but perhaps offering a little succor along the road.

"It's a wonderful idea," said my husband. "Just make sure everybody signs a waiver at the gate."

9

Wool, Milk, and Company

Route 9 runs between Northampton and Amherst. It was for most of my youth a two-lane road with farms on both sides. But this changed quickly in the 1970s, when the University of Massachusetts underwent its fantastic expansion and created a virtual metropolis in the middle of the corn fields. Route 9 became a series of malls, minimalls, chain restaurants, gas stations, pizza parlors, motels, traffic lights, and traffic jams. The town of Hadley, through which this unsightly stretch of roadway now goes, was clobbered by ugliness. Bumper stickers were printed that read: HADLEY'S GOT YOU BY THE MALLS.

"Didn't we go somewhere around here to pick pumpkins?" I asked my father one October day as we were driving to South Hadley to pick apples. This was my first trip back to Northampton since the perturbing experience at the Agway.

"Yes," he said. He looked to his left. "Oh. They've made it part of the parking lot for that set of stores."

"Mall."

"Yes, I guess it is a mall. Well, that paved area, behind it, that's where the pumpkin field used to be."

"You know," he added, "the asparagus never came back to

this valley. I hear the fungus problem stays dormant in the soil."

Ever since I became involved in agriculture, my father has taken up the subject with a fervor. He reports to me on what he finds at the Saturday farmers' market in town. He cuts out relevant articles for me from *The New York Times*. He interrogates orchard owners, livestock producers, and specialty mushroom growers whom he finds along his path. I took him to a sheep festival one weekend, and apart from the excessive bleating he had a good time. He even bumped into people he knew that he never realized had sheep.

I know my father worries about whether the farm will "be enough" for me, whether it will challenge and satisfy me sufficiently. He has identified me differently for so long: as a businesswoman, and as a writer and poet. But he is still ready to get excited with me about this farm, and he is already thinking out new recipes for the yields.

Of course, I also have the spirited encouragement of my husband, who, like my father, thinks of farming and grilling in one breath. While my father is open to whatever animals and crops (parsnips, please) I choose, my husband has shown some distinct partialities. He has a penchant for sheep, a penchant that comes from we know not where. He likes their habits and attitude, and he regularly champions the practical aspects of their size—compared to, say, a thousand-pound feedlot steer.

"Now think about it," he said one day as we watched the bison herd at the Bronx Zoo tear apart their morning ration of hay bales. "Could you throw a steer in the back of the pickup if you had to move him? Take him to the vet's? But a sheep, well, I just wouldn't have to worry about you. They're a good size for you, I think."

I took my husband to a sheep festival in New York State and he nearly bought four breeding ewes at the auction. I was grateful, for both his enthusiasm and his restraint. We looked over a variety of breeds, and we both prefer the Suffolk. Suffolk sheep stand tall and muscular, with a beautiful spring of girth and a graceful line to their legs. We were also taken by their black faces, the Roman noses, and the quiet temperament of the Suffolk ewes we saw in the show ring.

There are some less charming aspects to consider with sheep. They require constant worming, for example. They graze very close over the grass and often too near to their own droppings, and to my mind that bespeaks an animal with a virtual partiality to infection. Among most breeds, religious "crutching" of the breeding ewes is imperative. Crutching refers to the shearing of the wool from their back quarters and teat area to make suckling more manageable and hygienic for the newborn lamb. Moreover, sheep tend to pull grass up by the roots, so pastures must be assiduously managed. Some neighbors up the road once asked me to find them some sheep to "warm up" the meadow behind their house. These were sheep, not for eating, but for entertaining. I made a few inquiries, but the project was instantly halted when my neighbors were informed by a friend that sheep would ruin their lovely lawn by grazing it too short.

Many people show a fondness for and satisfaction in the greasy, dirty, lanolin-thick wool. My husband adores the voluminous angelic curls of a Rambouillet's fleece. We have been amazed to watch these long-haired varieties get sheared—out of a sumptuous mantle of oily, yellow-white wool steps a skinny, forlorn pink body. Still, I have been undecided about keeping a significant number of sheep on my farm, and I realize that some of my hesitation comes from having visited lambing enterprises where the animals were poorly cared for. There I have found sheep mired in mud and, overall, a grubby lot.

"We don't have to do it that way," coaxed my husband. "I've seen clean sheep . . . well, relatively clean sheep. But we won't have to worry about washing the wool anyway. We'll be shipping it off for processing, won't we? We can just worry about the racks of lamb."

I accused him of being a lobbyist.

"You'll be glad I was," he said. "You won't be able to resist my sheep."

"Your sheep?"

"You're already jealous," he said.

I had to admit there were some fine points about raising sheep. They were not smart creatures, but they were agreeable enough. Easy to handle. Not too noisy. Not too aggressive. As a knitter, I liked the idea of producing wool, and my husband was obviously committed to enjoying his lamb. If we started with a flock of four pregnant ewes, I reasoned, we would have a few months to feel out the husbandry before their offspring started arriving. Moreover, ewes customarily twin once or twice a year, which is a producer's dream. Even so, I thought, the advantages of their fertility are slightly offset by their begrudging instincts for motherhood. Ewes often have to be trained first to acknowledge their own lambs and then to express any maternal attention whatsoever.

Are sheep cute? In my mind, yes, just after they have been sheared and they stand pink, naked, and miserable. And yes, newborn lambs are pretty ingratiating. Are they smart? Well, sheep breeders wriggle a little at that question.

"Smart in exactly what way?" They will probe you.

"Do you mean will the females exhibit a motherly inclination toward their lambs?" They will groan.

"Do you mean will this ewe seek shelter from the rain?" They will squint.

"Do you mean does this breed know a Border collie from a car?" They will kick at the gravel.

I spoke with one woman who said she had switched her flock over entirely to a breed called Montadales. They are short, stocky, wool sheep—as opposed to the larger, heavily muscled Suffolks, say, which are considered meat sheep—and she had both white and dark brown ewes to show at the sheep festival. The wool from Montadales has a lovely silky feel to it, and the yarn she had spun was more delicate, thinner than most. But the reason she chose Montadales was that they have, as a breed, little lambing difficulty, and they make good mothers.

"I work a full-time job during the day," she said. "I can't be rushing back to the barn every fifteen minutes to check for birthing problems. Montadales are very resourceful."

That remark really caught my notice. I had known that some breeds of sheep and cattle are notorious for having difficulty delivering, and I wanted to be sure I wasn't asking for that kind of trouble on my own farm. So I took a second look at this woman's Montadales, and indeed, they were pretty beguiling.

Montadales are a bit funny-looking. They have long, skinny faces nesting incongruously at the fore of a dense wad of wool. This wool creeps up their necks and comes to a dead stop just behind their ears, looking like an oddly ill-fitting turtleneck sweater. Their ears bolt out to the sides like airplane wings, and they will look at you with such bored glances, the ends of un-chewed grass sticking out from their mouths. "Ahhh," they chew at you, "so why don't you wanna be a sheep?"

My husband's enthusiasm has been contagious, if not plain persuasive. He tells me he has already planned "a perfect paddock" with an ample shed to protect the sheep from the weather. He has proposed setting up a new kind of charged wire fence that he read about. It is apparently both effective and easy to move for shifting sheep from pasture to pasture.

"It's from New Zealand," he beamed. "Now they should know."

He has even offered to plant a bountiful herb garden near the shed. "A few days before we send off a lamb," he strategized, "we can feed it nothing but rosemary, tarragon, and a little garlic . . ."

"I don't know if marinating works that way," I replied.

"You'll get to love them," my husband said.

He said, "We can call your farm Bleating Hearts."

The idea of having sheep around was winning me over. When

you have a farm operation—raising heifer calves, for example, or propagating rare livestock breeds—it's easy enough to keep a few extra sheep on the side. And there's always the possibility that what starts out as a farm sideline may mature into a whole separate enterprise. It's not difficult when you already have the barn, the hay source, the corn source, the pens. It's not inconceivable, I supposed, that I could even grow to find sheep enchanting. A pig farmer I met said he used to have an egg business—five hundred laying hens—and that he had always kept a few hogs around for the family. In 1987, when his egg business was suffering from prevailing cholesterol concerns, he had sold off his hens and bred his two Hampshire sows. Within two years, he had developed a healthy pork business. He gave me a tour of his barns, where hundreds of pink and striped and spotted pigs at various stages of development were padding around like happy busybodies.

"Well, I try to keep an open mind," I told him, "but I don't think I could get excited about keeping pigs."

"Only a farmer and a sow can love a pig," he said, tenderly scratching the grizzled hairs on the head of his young Duroc boar.

·

A wealthy friend of mine, Murray, once bought an incorrigibly lovable English Border collie for his daughter. Few people can dispute that affectionate puppies have some magnetic pull, and since Border collies are notably bright, their assault on the average human senses is overwhelming. This puppy was delivered to Murray's estate in New Jersey to the tune of much delighted screaming and hugging. But that didn't seem enough.

"It would be a tragedy," Murray explained, "to have this magnificent dog and not allow it to flourish within its natural instincts."

So Murray, to satisfy some internal reality, bought eight mature pedigreed sheep from a farmer in New York.

"To train the puppy," he said. "I've got some cassettes, a collar, and a manual, too."

Murray handed all these training materials over to one of his estate hands and pointed toward the sheep. I was lucky to have the chance to see these sheep when they arrived. They were Corriedales, considered a good dual-purpose breed—the lambs grow quickly, and the wool from females has a respectable value among the New England wool pools. Sure enough, they were beautifully conformed. Sheep, as I have mentioned, can rarely be found in any condition bordering on cleanliness (except in the show ring), but it was easy to see the quality in their frame and muscling. There were six females, all around two years of age, and two rams that were several months younger. It was a sunny April day when I watched them investigate their new environs at Murray's place. They were installed in a small pen beside his garage with a huge round bale of hay to nibble on.

"I buy only registered animals," Murray whispered to me in confidential tones. "Let me give you a piece of advice. Never, never buy an animal without papers. Never."

These eight sheep spent a few months browsing down through the mountain of golden hay as summer blossomed into a blaze of heat and flies. Once or twice a week, they would be led into a meadow behind Murray's house with the no-longer-such-a-puppy. There they were repeatedly harassed from fence post to fence post for an hour or so with no apparent motive on the part of the dog. Eventually Augie, the collie, would become bored with this game and leave his eight sluggish play-mates to graze in tenuous peace. I observed these peculiar training sessions over the course of July's steamy afternoons, and I wondered for whose benefit this exercise was being carried out. One day as I watched, Murray sauntered outside and leaned beside me on his comely split-rail fence.

"I don't get it," Murray said. "I think the guy that sold me those sheep was a crook. Registered junk is what they are. Do you see them out there? Here I've got this magnificent Border collie trying to herd eight heaps of wool. It's a tragedy," he said.

Murray's man was having a cigarette under a tree. The collie was barking and nipping at the hocks of the sheep who were grazing and stumbling forward now and then to escape the noisome harangue. I watched for a while and then turned to Murray.

"You know, Murray," I said, "I don't mean to intrude, but don't you think it's time to shear those poor sheep?"

"Shear them?" he asked. "Already? I just bought them."

"Yeah, I see your point," I mumbled, thinking, oh my God. It so happened that Murray was, in my book, not a man whose judgment one could lightly censure.

"But I think they're about to fall over dead from heat prostration, Murray. They're wearing about four fat inches of greasy wool and it's over eighty-five degrees outside."

Murray thought a minute.

"Maybe I should call the crook I bought them from," he said. "Tell him to take them back."

"My sense is, Murray," I said, "that your sheep are basically sound, but that in this condition they're not going to give Augie much of a challenge. I mean, that dog is really what it's about out there, isn't it?"

He thought back a well-groomed moment. "Of course," he replied.

"So maybe you could get one of your men to shear those unhappy bodies?"

"Maybe you're right," Murray said. His face furrowed a bit in thought. "Know who'd want to buy my wool?" he asked.

"No," I said. I wished I could have said yes. Murray went quiet.

Then he said, "Know anything about shearing sheep?"

The next time I visited Murray, the sheep were gone. Augie was out entertaining himself in the pachysandra patch, much to the chagrin of Murray's live-in groundskeeper.

"What happened, Murray?" I asked. "Where are your sheep?"

"Sold them," he said. "For next to nothing. And to the same swindler that sold them to me."

He sighed. "It's a tragedy. Those sheep were just pitiful— tired, sick, full of worms. Their hooves were rotting! Not as billed, you know what I mean? I should've looked more closely at those papers. I'm too naive. I trust people too much. I didn't expect that kind of double dealing from a farmer."

To me, Murray never made ignorance look like bliss. He made it look pretty objectionable. I was well aware that keeping a small flock of sheep was relatively effortless, and his inability to manage it made no mark on my determination to do so.

Sheep get along with rudimentary shelter, and you can get along managing them with a few pieces of practical equipment. Sheep don't require the constant pampering that horses may. They won't savage each other like chickens. They're not too big to handle in emergencies, and what's very convenient is that they're not difficult to find when you want to buy some. When I started looking around, I found a lot of small-scale sheep operations tucked within nearby suburbs and woods. For me this was a big advantage. Not only would it be easy to find ewes, but I had ready access to a local bevy of schooled farmers. I am a firm believer in talking to people in a business before I engage in that business myself. I know I'm not the first person to confront a new or problematic situation, so I like to hear what others before me have encountered and concluded. So many typical mistakes lie along a solitary path; my feeling is, even when I want to be a lone cowboy, I don't want to be a typical lone cowboy.

Farmers tend to be open about their experiences, their good luck and bad. They are the preeminent sources for information on how different breeds fare in your area, where to purchase your feeds, and which feeds are most reasonable. They can tell you where they bought their fencing and why they chose wood, say, over wire. They may recommend a vet in the region or a particular worm dip that seems the most successful. On the whole I think it puts you in better stead to introduce yourself early, let them know you're going to be raising a few sheep yourself, and ask their opinions on a thing or two before any paddock emergencies materialize and you're forced to introduce yourself panting with distress at their farmhouse door. It's common courtesy.

"So you wanna raise sheeps, do ya?" said one Maine sheep farmer to me with a big grin. "For meat or for wool?"

"I'm not sure yet," I said, preferring to sidestep the rare-breeds concept altogether.

"Well," he said. "I kun tell ya it ain't easy."

"I think I'm expecting that," I said. "But I'm going to do it anyway. How long have you been raising sheep?"

"Me? Me? Well, lemma think. Mebbe near on forty year or so. I kun certainly tell ya a thing or two, if ya was interested."

"I very well am interested," I piped up. "I'd really like to ask you a thing or two."

"Ah, would ya?" he said. He had very thick scraggly eyebrows that lifted with surprise momentarily off his eyes.

"I'd like to know," I smiled, "for instance, why you're raising Suffolks here. And I'd really like to know what you feed them."

"Ah, so, would ya?" He thought a minute. "Well, me, I got inta Suffolk for meat. I kunna get enough money from wool up hereabouts. People don't wanna trouble witht anymore, and I kun understandt. As for feed, well t'all depends on where ya farmst. For me, I got a fella down the road here, with a big, big hay operation. And I got my protein comin' from Bangor."

"Corn?" I asked.

"Yuh corn," he said. "Sommat beans, sommat pellet, sommat oats. Come on here, I'll show ya my barn."

We walked together into a huge wooden barn that had a cool, cavernous feel. I did a quick cross-check for bats and saw cobwebs dangling from the ceiling like stalactites. There was a pathway down the middle. On the left, three large paddocks had been set up using low wood fencing. Here were the market lambs, segregated by age and marked on their rumps with a splash of red, green, or blue to identify their sires. On the right was a work area complete with shearing machine and tilt squeeze, and behind it a sea of tiny lambing pens. In these small pens the farmer kept his breeding ewes and what he called his "mother-pens." We walked along the thin corridors between the pens and saw pregnant ewes panting, newborns groping for a teat, twinned and triplet lambs sleeping deeply in curls beside one another. Then we came back toward the tilt squeeze, which was painted bright red and seemed new.

"Do you have much occasion to use the squeeze?" I asked.

"Nuh," he said, and waved it off. "But muh vet, wall, he wuldna touch a ewe w'out. Just took the sheet offt yesterday, while muh vet comt today ta look uver a mum da kunnot stand."

The tilt squeeze is a sheep-size piece of equipment used for examination or treatment of an animal. In its simplest form it consists of a plywood board on one flank and an adjustable steel barrier on the other. Farmers sandwich the sheep snugly and can then rotate or tilt the contraption so as to have better access to the animal's hooves, for example, for trimming. Many sheep raisers I met owned one of these tilt squeezes, but few used them regularly. Sheep offer you the remarkable dexterity of standing still for handling, now and then.

"Nuh here's a fine dam," said the farmer, bringing us to a stop beside one of the mother-pens. "Gut a call frum a mun in Vermont, wunts me ta embryo transfer this 'un. Wunts to buy all the females. I think it over, I tell this mun. But I wun't."

"Why not?"

"Dun't wunt to charge her," he said. "She's dun enough. She dun't need no shots and flushin'. She's a good mum."

There were feeders of varying homemade construction styles scattered about. They were rudimentary V-shaped racks filled with hay and grain and pelleted feeds. The sheep stood beside them, poking their noses through the slats to pull out mouthfuls of this or that. Also dispersed around the corrals were mineral

blocks and long, galvanized iron water troughs set up on legs.
I had read that sheep drink around two and a half gallons of
water each day, but most of the animals in this barn, I noticed,
were contentedly gathered around the feed troughs.

Outside the barn was another paddock with three rams pacing
around. This paddock was connected with a series of fenced
meadows by means of portable, maneuverable "cutting chutes."
Cutting chutes are just fenced pathways wide enough for a single
animal abreast; they are used often throughout a farm to move
and sort animals one by one. This farmer had the chute arranged
so that he could drive his rams into specific meadows at breeding
time. It was a neat arrangement.

"Now what's that?" I said, pointing to an isolated, oversize
cement trough on the side of the barn.

"Muh dip," said the farmer. "But it's nah dry as bone now.
Havnt dipped since, ah, then, two month or so. Hate to dip.
Allas a mess."

The dip or dipping vat is a primitive but effective way to treat
sheep for lice, ticks and other assorted bodily bugs. Farmers fill
their vats with water mixed with medication and send the sheep
through, splashing, one at a time. It's not considered an amusing
chore and many farmers prefer spray guns loaded with the
proper compounds to this bathtub technique for delousing their
herd.

"I kun recummendt you," said the farmer, "thut you keep
yere barn clen. I wuld have to say, wall, dippin' is a most ent-
terrible task."

•

My strong inclination toward goats is well known among my
friends. They find it eccentric, I notice, because they feel goats
offer up no marketable products for today's society—goat's milk
and *cabrito* having no distinguished star within the red
Michelin—and they think goats have diabolical eyes. Still, they
say, they have been willing to overcome their countless reser-

vations and are always on the lookout for me when it comes to farm-related goings-on. Such a friend of mine, who lives in New York City, telephoned one day to recommend that I visit the Central Park Zoo.

"I'm sure I saw some goats there," he said. "Unless I was dreaming it. But goats aren't the kind of thing I usually dream about. Girls I dream about."

"Do you want to come along?" I asked.

"No thanks," he said. "I actually prefer dreaming about girls."

I made a trip to the park to find these goats and to see if the zoo had procured some unique breed for their exhibition. The Central Park Zoo, narrowly rescued amid New York City's recent budgetary crisis, was given a radical facelift a few years ago. It now boasts lots of wood and glass, carpeting, and unobtrusive walkways, reproduction tropical rainforests, pleasant open-air spaces, and opportunities to draw near to various animals. You can watch ants underground, seals underwater, and monkeys undercover.

Walking down Fifth Avenue toward the Sixty-fourth Street entrance, I began to pass by some zoolike (or miniature golflike) configurations on my right, beyond and below the brick wall that keeps you out of Central Park and gives the city's homeless at least one of four walls by which all human beings gauge a home. The brick wall was stained with urine and appropriated by intermittent bundlings of soiled blankets and ruined clothes—with warm bodies underneath. Homeless human beings left to live at the curb of a zoo created a compelling juxtaposition for me. At least those lions and tigers, I thought, have food and shelter from the weather.

I looked over the Sixty-sixth Street wall onto a strange pastel-colored concrete igloo, oversize, with several cement outcroppings. Beyond its railings were a cement whale poised in no water, and cheerful little kiosks that were empty, offering information to no one.

"This was the old zoo," a passing policeman informed me. "I don't think anybody uses it anymore." He glanced over the site. "No, I don't think so."

It seemed deserted. Its pastels and fairy-tale creatures suggested a happier time, like the now hushed pathways of the old World's Fair grounds. VISUALIZE COMPLETE ABANDONMENT, the bumper sticker would say. I was reflecting on this stark emptiness, disheartened, when suddenly three small goats appeared from behind the pink cement igloo. They were pygmy goats, short, dark-haired and friendly, and they jumped up onto the concrete bulges of the igloo wall as if they were scampering along the Matterhorn. They were an image of gaiety and self-contentment within this ungracious setting. I watched them play together—something goats do affably—and reexplore their cramped space. They sniffed without prejudice at the stray flotsam of Fifth Avenue and kept their hooves nicely trimmed by scampering about their lumpy concrete confines.

Goats are bright, gregarious, and engaging. They will wilt if left alone, but can manage very well with a companion of their own species, or a sheep, or a dog, or you. The goats in the Central Park zoo did not cry out at passersby for attention or deliverance, but rather chewed their feedstuffs in a copacetic manner in the midst of these hideous surroundings of cement and street litter. This reminded me of the way wildflowers buoyantly grow out of rock crevices.

In the goat vernacular, there are does (females), bucks (intact males), wethers (castrated males), and kids (goats under six years of age). Wethers make wonderful pets—not the kind of pet you want to jog with on the beach, but the kind that offers company, follows you as you tend the lawn, eats your grass clippings, nudges you in the side for an occasional break of stroking and scratching. Male or female, goats are experts at getting out of gates, into feed sacks, onto car roofs, and over fences. My favorite goat, a doe on a dairy farm in New York, was killed when she found some rat poison bars while climbing around a hayloft. Goats are naturally inquisitive and they are often smart enough to satisfy their curiosity, even when it's dangerous to do so.

Bucks are typically kept in a separate corral on goat farms because of their disposition, or lack thereof. Bucks with horns can be dangerous even without intending to be. And bucks have extraordinarily pungent pheromonal blast furnaces that keep them smelling just like an overripe chèvre. While it must drive the does to near distraction, it is not equally enamoring to the farmer.

Goats bond well with human beings. They can be greedy for petting and nuzzling. They tend to browse on all sorts of leafy and prickly plants and shrubs that no one else in the barnyard will touch—including poison ivy. But goats eat more than this-tles and scrub greenery. Many past owners of goats will rage at you. "I had goats!" they will curse. "See that meadow? Used to be fenced in. They ate down the fence and then they went after my apple trees."

The characteristic investigative palates of goats are celebrated in those terrific stories of devoured tin cans, tires, and little girls' dresses. In truth, a goat's curiosity may occasion a sniff or nibble, but neither their jaws nor their stomachs could manage such items. The story of the tin cans has more to do with a goat's predilection for the glue that binds a can's paper label than with the can itself. However, the appetite of a goat can in fact tackle a tree. It just takes time. It takes patient and determined gnaw-ing. Goats will chew away a ring of bark and wood about the height of their comfortable nuzzling, and few trees can survive this girdling procedure. That, finally, is how goats will "eat" your trees.

If you want conversation on your farm, buy goats. Goats you can talk with about subjects ranging from the Reagan admin-istration (which in retrospect probably gave older goats a bad name) to the quantities of hay that you are offering on any given day. Goats will hear you out about your most personal grievances, too, like your friend's inability to control her child or your family's reluctance to see you as other than an infant. I have felt silly talking to a lot of animals—even cooing to them at times—but with goats I always feel adequately heard. They remind me some of dogs, intelligent dogs, usually those medium-size mongrels that stray into your life now and then to keep you balanced.

I nearly bought two wethers one day from a convent not far from our cottage in Connecticut. The convent was perched on the top of a broad and scenic hill, and at the foot of that hill the nuns had built a modest farm from which they produced enough meat, milk, and eggs to satisfy the whole convent and then some. Within the small barn area, mapped into carefully prescribed and managed paddocks for the various resident species, Sister Margaret and Sister Lucy kept five dairy cows, ten sheep, five goats, one buck, more than thirty laying hens, and probably a matching number of barn cats and kittens. I used to drive over now and then to watch the animals. It's great to be able to visit other farms and enjoy someone else's animals. It's like being an aunt—you get all the pleasures with none of the ultimate responsibilities. I haunted the convent also to find out what the sisters were offering by way of seasonal feeds, shelter, breeding, and day-to-day attentions. I admit I was intractably predisposed to think these nuns would make the best farmers. It wasn't because they were women, but because they seemed like such a placid and do-unto-others lot. They were also, it was clear, hefty and fit enough to take on any of the larger animals—not that one is normally pressed to "throw" a dairy cow.

The goats there were of mixed parentage. They were tall, not the pygmy variety that I have often found in the Northeast— in light, I suppose, of space constraints. These convent goats reminded me of giraffes, in that they had long skinny necks springing up from a central, horizontal nucleus of stomach and ribs. Four disproportionately skinny legs wobbled underneath, looking deceptively weak. As they walked, this central expanse of chest-to-rump swayed like a flirtatious pair of hips, side to side. Then they would stop, stomach to one side, posed like Baroque angels in the idealized S-curve of a seventeenth-century triptych.

But there was more to that barrel-vaulted torso than grace. These goats adored attention and had a habit of strolling up to you and then shifting their weight suddenly, so that the whole horizontal force of stomach, muscle, and balance came slamming, affectionately, into your own imperfectly constructed (only two feet) verticality. Over you went unless you were accustomed to their ways. I think I could have invented the wrecking ball or the battering ram, way back when, by observing this effectively leveraged swing of the goat.

The taller breeds of goat are quite elegant. They have elongated necks, a stately upright posture—goats never slump—and an affinity for staying clean. The bucks, with their sage's beards and lofting backward springs of horn, act like reserve princes of the barnyard even though they are often penned in small, removed quarters due to their strength and the strength of their incredible fragrance.

"When you handle a buck," said Sister Margaret with a beatific smile, "you will smell of chèvre until Sunday."

I told my husband.

"We may have finally found something that clings worse than cigarette smoke," he said. "You'll have to stay off public transportation for a while, but we can certainly plan our vacations around your goat breeding cycles."

He said, "Tell me about this odor."

"No," I muttered.

"Maybe," he grinned, "it is more aptly termed a reek, or a stench even?"

I said, "It's a bouquet."

"We should bottle it then," said my husband. "I'm sure food

scientists could use it, if not the special forces of the U.S. Army."

Thus was my frame of mind vis-à-vis goats when kidding season at the convent farm began. It was a heyday for me, since there are few things so delightful as a baby goat; they are perky, approachable, more antelope than barnyard stock. I became happily attached to two twinned wethers whom I named Bob and Camel.

But Sister Margaret told me one morning that the convent couldn't keep all the spring calves, lambs, and kids, and that they planned to sell what animals they could to area farmers or families. I telephoned my father.

"Bob and Camel?" asked my father.

"Yes, and the nuns can't keep them," I said. "They're going to sell them. You want two goats?"

"Hmmm," he said tactfully. "I don't know how I could. I'm away too often. And I would worry about neighborhood dogs."

"Yeah, I understand."

"And I couldn't milk them," he added. "I think you need a stronger back for that."

I said, "Bob and Camel are men."

·

One year I drove up to the Vermont State Fair in Barre. It was being held in what appeared to be a high school complex up on a hill in the middle of town. In one building that looked like a surrendered gymnasium were all the tractor and equipment dealers with their shiny new models—"a must for every farmer," not to mention "the incredible trade-in values I can offer you . . ." In the school itself, which would never smell the same again, were all the various farmers with their prize yields and livestock. A maple syrup contest spanned the whole first floor, and was hard to pass by. There were maple syrups from amber to dark, maple cream, maple candies, maple cookies, maple bread, maple pies, and maple milk. There were maple syrup makers conferring on the habits of their trees, the running of the sap that spring, the proper temperatures for candy production, and of course the sorry prices for their syrup in general.

Following my nose, I headed toward the basement. The odor of straw, hay, and manure got stronger with every turn of that inimitable public school staircase. I had forgotten how hard it used to be to want to learn in those drab, institutional schools of the 1950s. The goats and sheep I found down the stairs seemed equally nonplussed.

There were three Nubian milking does standing comfortably but still in a makeshift iron-bar pen. Half a bale of hay sat behind them, falling open little by little at the edges like a toppling deck of cards. A handful of bright orange carrots lay untouched on the straw. The goats occupied their space with reserve, thoughtfully chewing cud and looking out at the visitors to the fair— observer observed. One sensed that they felt the walls of their alien pen were not sufficiently dependable to protect them from the primitive hordes walking by. MILKING AT 3:00 P.M., read a hand-scribbled sign on the wall behind them. It had been taped to the painted cinderblocks, and now hung—since tape has no adherence to these surfaces, and the frustrations of elementary school art classes came flooding back—limp, curling, and askew.

Nubians are one of the larger goat breeds, and they have a proud stature. The ones at the fair were cream and white colored with a patchy, mottled mix of the two shades and a hint of tan.

"You interested in Nubians?" said a cheery woman behind a card table. She had been serving up fresh goat's milk to passersby in the tiny plastic cups that doctors use to dish out pills.

"Yes," I smiled. The goats slowly swung their heads in my direction with a weary "and-who-are-you?" expression.

"Should be!" she said. "Nubians are the queens of goat breeds. Don't give as much milk, maybe, but the butterfat content's always higher than the others. Here, try some of our milk."

I took a sip of the cooled, sieved milk, and caught my breath. It tasted awful. Bitter, thick, not right. I couldn't seem to swallow it. It hung in the back of my mouth. My throat was saying *Non, mais absolument non.* I had to use all the coercive, rational powers of my brain to get it down.

"Thank you," I must have coughed, trying my best to be courteous and holding onto the tiny cup as though I fully intended to indulge myself in another sip.

"It's not a taste for everyone," she said, gaily ignoring my efforts. "Do you like goat's cheese, though? We've got some for sampling that we make ourselves."

"That would be wonderful. How old are your goats?"

"These does are all two years old," she said. "Frankly, I think it was a big mistake to bring them. The older does do better at these sorts of fairs—not so put off by all the people. These girls won't eat until everyone goes, which, you know, is kind of late. I asked my partner to go get some oats and molasses, see if we could get them to eat treats. He should be back soon. It's always like this at shows. There's always something you plan wrong."

I inquired about her farm.

"We've got over sixty acres in pasture and hay production just southwest of here. Goats are ruminants, of course—did you know that? Good. Well, we produce all our own roughage and buy oats or corn or soybeans for protein. The usual stuff. We've got about sixty does milking at any one time, and maybe fifteen drying off. It certainly wasn't like this a few years ago. I mean, we started out pretty small, but goats have twins more often than not, and lots of our does are having triplets, so we've grown faster than we planned.

"It's okay, though. We worried about having too much milk and where would we sell our kids and you know, but it's worked out okay. There's a lot of people around interested again in goat's milk for ice cream or for their kids. We got into cheese ourselves, not knowing what else to do with all the milk, and cheese is where the profit is with our herd. We're not fancy breeders or anything. We've got no purebreds to sell, no semen from our bucks. Our cheese, though, gets better every year."

"It's delicious," I said. It was. I wondered who might be selling baguettes and wine at the Vermont State Fair so that I could round up a nice picnic for myself. Vermont wine? I wondered. It was a chilling proposition.

I asked, "Does cheese-making involve a lot of new equipment and overhead?"

"No, not for us. Not yet." She paused. "Well, we haven't got into all the fancy machines. But since we already had a dairy parlor and sterilizing equipment, the added mechanics weren't to speak of. Where we really needed help was know-how. We didn't know the first thing about cheeses, other than how to unwrap them from the store. If you're interested, there's an old guy up in Saint Albans that taught us how, still gives us tips from time to time and even showed us how to shape the pyramids and ash the cheeses. He was incredible. A French guy. You should meet him. But don't talk to him until you've tried yourself a time or two. He can be kind of impatient unless you know what you're trying to do."

She gave me his name and address and I said I looked forward to the opportunity to be snapped at.

"By the way," I said. "What do you feed your goats besides hay, carrots, oats, and molasses?"

"Well." She took a big breath and launched into a discussion of the proper balance between roughage and protein and kitchen scraps and feed supplements, pounds of energy per lactating doe versus pounds of energy per dry doe, today's cost per pound of corn and soybeans, and so on.

Wait a minute, I thought. Somebody talk bales to me.

Over by the sheep pen a crowd was gathering, so I finished up chatting with this woman, thanked her, and walked over to have a look. Three sheep, all Rambouillet ewes, were ambling around an unglamorous pen erected from old wood planks while three infant lambs slept in the straw. The lambs were offspring from one of the ewes, who was identifiable from her cleanly crutched rear end. The farmer who owned these animals had just stepped into the pen to give a hoof-trimming demonstration, and I could see from his face that he rued this commitment. The sheep were altogether discombobulated by the fair, the lights, this temporary dormitory, and the milling crowds. "On any other day," was the edict of their agitated tramping, "but my hooves stay on the ground this morning."

The farmer stood still a while watching the ewes scuttle about. I imagined he was trying either to calm them or to calculate his chances at snatching one as she trotted by. Suddenly, he lunged forward and tried to collar a passing hock with his hand. *Blaaaaaah,* came the response, plus two sharp tugs of her leg and she was gone. And she was not, definitely not, going to circle by him again. And she was recommending to her friends, through a long series of loud bleats, that they follow her example. So nestle they all did against the opposite end of the pen.

Most of us watching this exercise, and enjoying it, thought the farmer had an easy shot now. Three fat woolly ewes cramming up against one another in a fairly tight space—all he had to do was catch one. He walked slowly over toward the ewes, working no magic but, on the contrary, bringing them to a pitch of sheep alarm. They broke, darted. He bent and reached. But before his arm had finished its swing they were behind him.

"More people should see this," said a man next to me. "Sheep will make you insane. I can't watch this anymore." And he shimmied backward out of the crowd.

Now the farmer was making low, soothing clucking noises —soothing to sheep, apparently, because they lowered their decibels and stood idle and examined him, their mouths relaxing into an indolent chew of cud. The mother ewe sauntered over to her lambs and poked one, as ewes will, exhibiting no tenderness but instead a kind of self-assertive reaffirmation. She watched, we all watched, as the farmer pulled a pair of pruning shears from his back pocket. Then he walked right up to her, squatted by her rear haunches, and picked up a hind leg. She complied.

"Sheep love foreplay," came a voice next to me. "But that's all they love."

The farmer straddled the ewe's upturned leg and gave the crowd a view of it. It seemed overly padded and had obviously grown outside the bounds of the original form. The farmer used his pruning shears to trim off slowly the areas of hoof that looked curled over. Then he took a knife from another pocket and began to shave downward, heel to toe, the rounded bottom portion of the hoof pad. Chunks of hoof were dropping into the straw. The farmer pulled back finally and showed us a tidy, trim, pinkening foot. "Well done"s and "There, he did it fine"s were circulating through the audience. Our farmer-performer put down the ewe's hoof and straighted his back, not without a wince.

"If anybody's got a question . . . ," he said.

But no, we'd seen enough.

·

Goats are the only farm animals that for me enter the gray area between livestock and pet. When I think about goats, the corners of my mouth curl up and my eyes drift skyward and I detect all sorts of words issuing forth from my mouth that I normally try to steer clear of—words like *cute, sweet, frisky, snuggly, fuzzy, nuzzly* (a word, even?), *cuddly,* and the like. This kind of jargon, apart from being really soupy and brainless, exposes me, the budding farmer, in a high-risk category—High Risk Of Not Being Able To Differentiate between barn and home, between Angus dam number 82 and Pheephee the house cat, between animals for food and animals for companionship. The dividing factor, of course, is the packing plant. We Americans don't eat dogs and cats. We don't eat much *cabrito* (goat meat) either, but we don't have many friends with pet wethers and does. All of us draw our curious lines, and we usually have good reasons for it.

On my farm, goats will largely be guests, in that I don't intend to support the local specialty meat market, the local goat's milk ice cream market, or the local mohair wool market (mohair comes from Angora goats). That said, I may be willing, every so often, only at the behest of the best of friends or family, and with reluctance, to have a male kid allocated for meat. I would also consider milking a small number of goats, were there an expatriate Frenchman in the neighborhood with a passion and an extraordinary genius for making fresh chèvre and an un-Frenchmanlike generosity of spirit that embraced a cheese-for-milk barter arrangement. And, in spite of the fact that Angora goats are renowned for their nasty temperament, I might keep a few around for the sake of a discourse in varietals.

Angora goats grow to just midthigh (mine) height. They are a spectacle in their full-length coat of crinkly white hair. Many breeders I have watched will lead their Angora goats into the show ring by grabbing them by the short curl of horn and then practically dragging them across the straw and dirt to position. It's a comic scene: twenty or so breeders between the ages of eight and fifty-eight, all decked out in cowboy boots and bandannas and each crooked over at the waist with two hands firmly wrapped around one horn of a contrary Angora goat—the goat, spanking clean and shimmering with its just-shampooed mohair locks, with four trimmed hooves bolted into the dirt and an expression of convincing opposition that could only come from genetics.

Something there is, for me, that loves a goat. But I watch myself closely with goat conversation. I try to monitor my language carefully. I try to expunge most of the "adorable"s from my sentences. And this is not just because I am busily training myself to the proper imprint of a farmer; I have always been uncomfortable with things considered "cute."

"Repressed," said a friend. "Repressed about things that are cute. You should know that, of all people. You're the psychiatrist's daughter."

"Psychoanalyst," I said, deadpan. I am tired of the "psychiatrist's kids" quips after all these years; I tend to think most everyone carries with them both the banners and the baggage of their parents.

Nevertheless, cute things introduce a level of discomfort into my life. I grew up equating cute with fatuous, cute with intolerable triteness. I can't stand Hallmark cards. It makes me uptight to watch people make overt flurries over kittens, puppies, and other infant species that normally draw out the cuddling instincts in one. When I was a child, people still avoided "scenes" or "making a scene"—which certainly dates me in the face of America's current day utterly unrestrained codes. And within our household, to indicate a partiality for the color pink was to risk excommunication from the family.

Everyone grows up under the doctrinal cudgels of their parents' and their society's moralities. I wear the expected dents about me. I hope I carry a smaller cudgel. Today I am immeasurably grateful for having been shepherded through my childhood to grasp education as my first priority. It was indeed the scholarly canons of my youth that taught me how to continue forward and greet life during my mother's long illness and after her death.

But it is farming that is my balm. It is the unceremonious work of the hands and spine in a day-to-day continuum that brings me repose. A graduate student from Georgia once said to me as he led me through his Texas A&M groundnut research plot: "You know, peanuts are truly a tonic." I suppose that, for myself, farming is truly a tonic. And of course, with respect to goats, I'll be able to find them wholly cute and adorable within the privacy of my own barn.

10

The Fine Feathered
Cannibals

 "Would you mind terribly if I didn't read your chapter on chickens?" asked a friend one morning.

A curious question.

"I'm just sick to death of hearing about them," she said. "One horror story after another. Salmonella. Inhumane farms. Do you know I've switched butchers twice because of chickens?"

"No," I said. "And I don't mind." Thinking, I don't really mind, but isn't it funny how people have to make these public avowals. We were quiet for a moment.

Then I proposed, "I bet a lot of people feel the way you do. Maybe I shouldn't include a poultry chapter at all."

"What? Of course you have to. Every farm has chickens and turkeys wandering around. That's what gives a farm"—my friend considered—"proper farm atmosphere."

She added, "Besides, you've said you're already short-changing pigs—"

"Swine," I corrected her.

"You can't just keep leaving animals out. Why don't you write a short chicken chapter, and while you're at it throw in a little something nice about pigs for other people. Try to be diplomatic."

"Once upon a time there was a pig sty and a chicken coop," I said.

"Exactly."

I said, "Actually, I've been thinking a lot about chickens recently."

"Good attitude."

"About why we are so untroubled by slaughtering them."

"Oh God."

I had happened to be reading one of my husband's war history books at the time. In it the author proposed that it was easier to do battle with—that is, to kill—a person who looks least like you. Came the theory then, and I'm sure it was not unprecedented, that it was easier for Americans to war with the Japanese in World War II or the Iraqis in 1990 than it might be, say, to fight another Western culture. I can't argue with that line of reasoning. People, like countries, have an innate element of nationalism that stems very deeply from an internal sense of familiarity and community. Persons who look significantly different from us are more vulnerable to our instinctive tendency to find a safe and protective distance for ourselves.

"This is where I expect the NAACP to take a less than genial interest in your farm views," said my friend.

"I was trying to relate this to chickens," I said. "No chicken nuggets eater cares what color the original hen's skin was—although I guess you could argue that one should."

She said, "Oh, do they really make chicken nuggets out of chicken these days?"

For some reason, I think, it has been easier for Americans to accept the killing and eating of chickens than the same treatment of other livestock—calves, for example. Ah well, you're saying, calves are babies, and nobody wants to eat a baby. Okay, I'll say, suppose you're right, and let's forget the issue of eggs or lamb; my point is that human beings seem to be better able to distance themselves from birds than from other mammals. Put that way, it makes a lot of sense. Speciation. Birds are small, armless, fluttery, jerky creatures, with none of that big brown eye stuff in their favor. They are rarely approachable, they make curious squawks, and their standard of hygiene is less than we like to imagine. They grow to adulthood in a matter of weeks, they aren't particularly precocious, and you can't pet them with satisfaction.

For all of these reasons, I think chickens are more readily taken into the pan than into the heart. The entire chicken industry has survived many a discouraging word over the matter of salmonella, chickens' dietary habits, their cannibalistic propensities, and the densely packed grow-out barns in which they're raised. None of the mud seems to stick. Chicken consumption rose at a stupendous rate in the 1980s in spite of searingly bad press. I should like to be so popular as a 1980s chicken.

"I still don't see how you can translate that war theory into chicken consumption," resisted my friend. "Especially since human beings don't look much like cattle either. Well," she considered, "at least I hope I don't look much like a cow. Some of the people you see on the street, however . . ."

"Hold on," I said. "Listen to this." I had been flipping through a textbook titled *The Meat We Eat* (Interstate Printers & Publishers), and I found a section in the poultry chapter called "Handling Previous to Processing." It began: "Birds, like animals, should receive careful handling to avoid bruises, abrasions, and broken limbs."

"At least I think birds are animals," I said.

·

I like to watch chickens. I notice also that chickens don't mind being watched. They have a kind of feline independence to them. Their world is manageably circumscribed and you, other than around feeding time, are on the Outside. Within a microcosm of wood chips, lettuce leaves, and of course chicken wire, come the contenting patterns of their day—the laying of the egg, the scratching for the beetle, the roosting on a convenient branch, and the hunting up of a little more sunshine.

In 1989, I became acquainted with chickens while I worked on a small farm in Connecticut. It was mainly a beef cattle operation, but there were also sheep, poultry, pigs, and the seasonal duck. No one there liked chickens except for me. The other farm hands considered birds filthy, and moreover very filthy. I, however, was mesmerized by my first box of chicks and became completely attached to these birds by the time they became full-time egg layers or big-breasted broilers. The more I learned about them, the less charming they became in my mind, and the more amazing. I used to watch chickens during my coffee break, watch chickens as I thought through my reports, and watch chickens before I went home at night. They were bewitching and they were comic. They were curious about human beings but considered themselves smart enough to keep a safe distance from you.

One of my favorite moments of the farm day came every morning at ten o'clock. The laying flock was let out into the back meadow to spend some hours in the sun scratching the dirt for pebbles and bugs. The hens had finished laying their eggs in the nests (boxes built against the walls of the barn). They were ready to stretch their legs, and this interlude gave the farmhands time to collect warm eggs from the hay inside the coop.

This airing of the hens and roosters was a methodical routine interrupted only by sharp drops in the temperature, blizzards, rain, or hail. Chickens take well to schedules, to laying in the mornings, to wandering about during the daylight, to heading home at dusk. But in spite of the consistency of this daily custom, one step along the way invariably provoked alarm throughout the flock. This was the actual passage out of the barn through a tiny, bird-size door in the far wall of the coop. This little door opened out onto a ramp fixed to the rear of the barn. The ramp took the chickens down one storey to the ground and meadows beyond. Perhaps the problem was that the ramp ran parallel to the barn wall instead of jutting straight out perpendicular to it. This meant that the flock had to exit the coop and take a sharp right down the ramp. If a bird marched too far forward, it would have to do some flying—not something domesticated chickens are keen for.

So it was that when the little latched door of the coop was opened each morning, consummate havoc erupted. Hundreds of buff and white chickens, fussed at impatiently by those behind and pecked at by the member roosters, would begin shoving and bursting through the barn wall onto the ramp outside. Because the ramp was fairly slim—just wide enough to endure two fat chickens comfortably toddling side by side—each bird as it was pushed or crowded through the little door would suddenly panic as it greeted the sheer five-foot drop straight ahead. Every morning.

Chickens still do come with wings in these modern times, and yes, they can use them to buffer any free-fall. Even so, the march of the hens each morning amounted to ten minutes of unadulterated chaos and terrified squawking as the river of orange and white birds raged, surged, and spewed forth from the coop into the precarious sunlight. Most hens did manage to walk or be shoved down the wooden ramp, but a few inevitably got thrust off the side and would fall, not gracefully, to the ground. The air resounded with chicken umbrage and the minor thuds of birds landing abruptly on their breasts or rumps. Nothing was bruised, as it is said, but a modicum of dignity. The unfortunates would bounce up quickly, affronted, and forget the incident within seconds. Chickens, I think, have enviably small memory lobes.

"The brains have been bred out of 'em," said one chicken farmer to me. "It's easier to deal with 'em without brains."

I guess that would be true. It would be tough to be the warden of a wily freedom-seeking bird.

"Chickens weren't always so dumb and defenseless," he added.

"Used to use their wings more. Used to run faster, think better."

The road to the better meat and egg-laying bird was not parallel to the road to the fittest chicken. Sometimes I imagine the two trends are inversely related. If we were to let chickens revert, live freely in the wilderness, would we see a gradual return of their former cleverness or habits? Would they begin to bear offspring with a more astute and aggressive nature? And, I have wondered, would we ever see the gradual differentiation of the species back into its ancestral variations?

This is an important issue for me, since I hope to raise some of the older poultry races. I am nagged at by the thought that these races simply don't exist in any purity today, that we have only mongrel material on the hoof (on the claw, in this case), and some antique lithographs that reveal to us what a certain breed used to look like.

What's done, with chickens, is done. I think people kid themselves when they try to breed backward to the original, parental genetics, to what Darwin called the "aboriginal stocks." By raising a few of the older races, however, I hope to preserve at least some segments of the early genetic codes, and perhaps a few traits that, expressed or not in the remaining individuals, may continue to be passed along through careful breeding.

But whether you want minor breeds of poultry or major, ducks or chickens, you may be delighted to learn that they are relatively easy to come by. Modern day hatcheries will send you glossy catalogues with a wide selection of full-size chicken breeds, bantams, turkeys, water fowl, and guineas. You telephone in your order, tell the ladies what kind of chicks you want—if you want all pullets (females), cockerels (males), or a "straight run" (unsexed mix). Straight runs tend to be slightly less expensive. Then you must let the ladies know whether you want your day-old chicks vaccinated and/or debeaked. You should know that debeaking at this early stage is only effective for the first few weeks. Beaks keep growing, and if you plan to keep chickens in tight confinement then you may have to redebeak them some day yourself. Also, debeaked chickens can be a thoroughly woeful sight.

Depending on the hatchery, the type of poultry, and the number of chicks you order, the cost per chick can run from around forty-five cents to a couple of dollars. Exotic breeds naturally are the more expensive. Vaccination and debeaking will add another five cents or so to the cost of each chick. Visa and Mastercard numbers are often accepted over the phone.

At this point you should have your chicken starter and warm lights ready. A perforated cardboard box full of fluffy white or cream-colored chicks will arrive by overnight mail at your local post office, cheeping like crazy and straining the nerves of employees reared on mute parcels and backroom humdrum. The postmaster will call you up and let you know your chicks have arrived. Pick them up right away and get them to food and water. Baby chicks ingest enough of the egg's nutrient-rich yolk to last them about twenty-four hours after hatching, but then they need some care.

"Amazing," murmured a friend. "Chicks by mail order. I'm going to look differently at my L. L. Bean catalogues now."

·

People love eggs that get properly pipped, fractured, and pushed apart by a wet-feathered scrawny chick inside. They don't, anymore, love eggs that get rapped bowlside, cracked in two, and loosed into the frying pan. Conjuring eggs as carriers of salmonella, cholesterol, or unwanted calories, Americans over the last several years have been demanding more pipping and less rapping.

The egg business became a lousy business to be in during the 1980s—demanding, industrial, and ever under fire from book-writing nutritionists. It's still demanding and industrial, but there are signs that the nutritionists have retreated some. They appear to have a jungle war mentality, and, having laid waste to a few treehouses, they are on the lookout for booty in other

precincts—waffles, perhaps. Yes, waffles have not yet been pil-
loried. In the meantime, I was surprised when a series of favorable egg episodes, egg interludes, happened along my path.
The first story arrived with a friend from New York.

"You have got to see the new exhibit at the Whitney's Forty-
second Street gallery," she said. "It's all tempera painting. Tempera is in again. Everybody's into mixing up their own paint
pigments and separating out the egg yolks . . ."

A rash of tempera painting alone was not going to revive the
egg industry, but it was a modest effort. I called my sister the
art conservator.

"Oh!" she said. "It'll never last. It's painstaking. You mix your
pigment with egg yolk for binder. The effect on the canvas is
unusual but it's hard to work with. It dries very fast."

Soon after, I was looking for inspiration in a craft magazine
and I came across an article on herb-decorated boxes. Dried
herbs could be applied to wooden boxes with egg white, then
the whole thing lacquered. I tried it because I wanted to make
my husband something special to commemorate his prodigious
herb garden, and I was intrigued to see what an effective neutral
glue the egg whites made.

On balance then, yolks to the pigment-binding, whites to the
clear adhesives.

That same week, I went to visit Miss Card at the local nursing
home. Miss Card was one hundred and two years old, the last
surviving member of a family of nine children. She had grown
up on a farm in Ontario and each week credited her ongoing
longevity to the healthiness of that arduous but wholesome
childhood. When I visited with Miss Card we spoke typically
about her farm chores as a young girl. On this particular visit,
watching the trees bud outside her window, she recalled the
way her family would make maple syrup each year.

"We always used to tap our trees," she said. "We had big
caldrons boiling with sap, first the one and then into another.
We kept them outside, in the bush. And when the syrup was

still hot, we poured it through sieves to strain out the larger impurities. Then my mother mixed up some milk and egg and stirred it into the warm syrup. The mixture cooked in the heat of the syrup and rose to the surface, taking all the rest of the impurities with it, and we could just spoon it off the top. All the dirt and dusts attached to the egg and we could lift it off with our hands."

I was beginning to look at eggs quite differently by now, seeing them not just as the province of breakfast and baking but as fundamental apparatus throughout the home. It was then that my mother-in-law said, while sipping on some of my coffee, "The best coffee I ever drank was in Texas. I had a friend, Ann, and she had a pot made out of, well, the material that lines ovens. The blue and grey lining? Ann mixed the coffee grounds with hot water and then she always threw in a couple of egg shells. The shells brought the grounds to the bottom and the coffee on top was absolutely wonderful!"

"The egg shells brought the grounds down?" I laughed. "Surely that's a little Southern witchcraft."

"No," my mother-in-law said firmly. "It worked that way. I don't know why but it actually worked."

I believed my mother-in-law (one must), so I telephoned the American Egg Board in Chicago to ask them why this short-of-kitchen-miracle reaction would happen.

"Hmmmm," came a voice on the other end of the line. I noticed this woman also had a Southern accent, so I was sure I had reached the qualified party. "Egg shells in coffee," she said slowly in her drawl. "I'm just writing this down. Do you mind if I put you on hold one second?"

I didn't. She was not long gone.

"Just the shells?" she asked.

"Yes," I said.

"Do you happen to know whether they were crushed or intact?"

"No, I don't," I replied. "I hadn't thought to ask."

"Of course not," she said soothingly. "Do you mind if I put you on hold again?"

"No," I said. I hummed to their country tunes.

"Honey, you still there? I can honestly tell you I have never heard that egg shells bring down coffee grinds, but I'm sure if your friend said so then that's true. You know, eggs are truly marvelous things . . ."

I was beginning to feel the same way, I was going to say. Eggs were growing in stature in my mind, too, but I don't have a lot of patience with trade-group pitches, so I asked her to send me some materials and rang off. Enough of this omelette business, I was thinking. People should be able to buy eggs at the hardware store. You wouldn't need to worry about fat, cholesterol, and food poisoning when you used the egg for general purpose home maintenance.

This flurry of new ideas for egg use made me think more about all farm yields as perceived in the past. There used to be more one could glean from a carcass, more one could accomplish with an egg, more ways one could look at a plant. I was reminded of a history lesson way back in elementary school. We read thick, disintegrating text books describing how the Indians of the Great Plains killed only as many buffalo as they needed to survive. The meat they ate. From the hides they made clothes and teepees. From the skeletons they fashioned weapons and implements. They made thread, for sewing those clothes and teepees, from the sinews, and they made needles for sewing from the bones. This was one of those Good Indian lessons, you realize, to be differentiated from the more numerous (in my day) Bad Indian sermons about gratuitous scalping and innocent-settler slaying.

And now I was amazed to hear of a few innovative things to do with an egg—so far am I from having to be creative, so provincial am I about my foodstuffs. Today both producers and consumers of food share a very restricted approach to food production. We breed hens specifically for egg-laying or meat yield. At the end of their productive (and hopelessly unattractive) life—eggs adjourned, meat packaged—their remains are fit only for the U.S. Army's massive soup tureens, in which the vestiges can be safely dissolved without imparting too much flavor. The remnant feathers, bones, and entrails are sometimes metamorphosed into chicken feed themselves—a nicely circular if distasteful route.

Well, at least we Americans are not wholly prodigal. We may not use all parts of a livestock carcass to full therapeutic advantage, but we certainly don't waste what we don't directly eat. Very little, in fact, is wasted in the modern packing house. All the organs, bones, fat and blood that consumers won't buy get recycled into processed foods, animal feeds, medical and industrial uses. Many of the edible parts that you wouldn't think of selecting outright will turn up, in plastic, in the refrigerated meat section of your supermarket—diverted into processed food products you will indeed buy. Nay, pet food is not the only end of the line for unsavory organs.

There are plenty of industries that take the beef fat, grind up the chicken feathers, tan the hides, and otherwise dispose of the less edible portions of a carcass. It's an efficient way to deal with the plain tonnage of detritus left after the valuable meat cuts are removed, but it's not a system that can be sensitive or creative with specific bodily by-products. Feed manufacturers and not coffee connoisseurs want the world's waste eggshells, the mass flotsam from big egg processing factories.

The number-one unpleasantness in coping with mass in general, I think, is that it forces you to ignore the value of individual components. It compels you to average, to dilute, to compromise excellence with poor quality and to neglect the merits of constituent parts. This happens within our enormous chicken processing industry and it occurs throughout our society today in a multiplicity of areas. Our own population has grown so large that government policies and doctor's offices and airplane companies are forced to deal with us as one immense herd of kindred cattle. We are all processed daily, issued new client numbers, gathered, and moved. In the modern livestock industry, so many animal carcasses are pushed through the slaughter plant each day that the waste is much easier dealt with as one manageable heap than as a gross accumulation of exclusive and serviceable parts. Burn it.

Perhaps the only other nonfood industry that has made aggressive forays into the American refrigerator is the cosmetics industry. They're interested in egg yolks, too, I notice, but they haven't cramped themselves within any one food group. Advertisements tell me that I can buy soap with oatmeal in it, shampoo with wheat germ and honey lurking inside, avocado and cucumber facial masques, or beer and lemon elixirs for my hair. It makes me uneasy to think that people who someday buy my farm produce might be going home to a mortar and pestle and shower. I don't like the notion that I might end up supporting any self-beautification craze.

I talked with one of my sisters about the many forgotten uses of different carcass parts, and she instantly burst into laughter.

"You've got to have a kind of prairie-days mentality to look to food wastes as an arts and crafts reservoir," she said. "Please, don't tell me: You're going to ask your butcher which cut of lamb would be better for staining dining room chairs. Well, I'm not the one to talk to, Nora. Just looking at a cake of yeast makes me edgy. And, well, eggshells in my coffee?"

I couldn't tell her she had slipped irreparably over the precipice into drab modernity. Or if she had, I was skidding downhill beside her. The fact is, while one can be intrigued to learn the various and diverse merits of common farm products, it's not easy to incorporate many of them into contemporary life unless seized by a sudden fit of "green" ingenuity.

"If you want everything *but* the steaks from your farmyard," my sister went on, "be sure to let me know. I *only* want the steaks, so that's fine." She giggled.

"Oh, God, Nora," she said. "Are you going to raise eye-of-newt next?"

·

"Exciting news in the turkey department," I said to my husband one afternoon. I had been flipping through some mail and poultry magazines while he was assembling elaborate radios piece by piece on the kitchen table.

"Hold on a minute," he whispered, his nose among the curious array of little leather Mickey Mouse ears and color-banded knobs that he fuses into circuit boards. He finished a presumably exacting maneuver and then straightened his back. The strain of this operation, which he calls a hobby, was obvious.

"Try breathing," I smiled. "Is this a radio for my chicken coop?"

"Do birds like music?" he asked, eyebrows raised high with mistrust.

"When you find their ears, I'll tell you if they like music," I said.

"Okay," he laughed. "Now what's this about turkeys?" He is markedly patient with my outbursts.

"Dad sent me a flyer from a butcher shop announcing the sale of Bronze turkeys, and then by coincidence I just found an article in one of my journals which says they're gaining in popularity."

"Bronzed turkeys?" He crinkled his face. "This sounds like some nasty offshoot of the group that gold-plates baby shoes."

"No, no," I said. "It's a breed. It's a color."

"I see," he said, nodding. "That's terrific, is it?"

"It's terrific," I replied. "Why don't you solder a bit while I go downtown and check out our local butchers." I called up a friend of mine and we went together.

The Broadbreasted Bronze is steadily making a commercial comeback. With hindsight, I can say I should have expected as much. America's bored and affluent baby-boomers have made such an elite sport of uncovering every conceivable curious food on the planet—white asparagus from China's conical mountains, yellow raspberries, alligator meat, and so on. Their parents strove for the perfectly white bread, but this generation will only eat stone-pounded, gritty brown loaves. For their parents, turkey producers nationwide switched over to a white-feathered bird so that every Thanksgiving roast would have that perfect translucent skin. It was only time, I guess, before the kids said, "No thanks. Show me those dark-feathered turkeys that I see on the greeting cards. Show me a roast with black pin feathers."

"Now, tell me again, why do I want black pin feathers?" asked my friend as we drove downtown. "And what are pin feathers anyway?"

I had appointed myself her food fashions coach.

"Not to worry," I said. "Tiny tiny feathers that may still be lodged under the skin. You rarely see them on white-feathered birds, and if you did, well, they pretty much burn off in the oven anyway."

"I hope I have never eaten a feather!" she said. She was from the South. Northerners would probably eat feathers if they were properly promoted.

It's good to be warned about dark-feathered birds. Their appearance can be startling the first time. You might suspect even the most highbrow butcher of an egregious transgression when you spot a Bronze in his meat case—a massive ready-to-roast bird covered with dark needle-pricks and inky stains. In spite of forewarning, my friend's jaw fell open when we arrived at the butcher's and she hung out a limp finger in the direction of the glass case.

"You're trying to poison us," she said to the butcher. "This bird died of scrofula or the Black Plague or something."

The butcher rolled his eyes with that kind of reverse snobbism that seems to make Bergdorf Goodman clerks so prosperous.

"This is a turkey that had, when it was alive, brown and black feathers," he explained. "It is called a Bronze, and the bronze turkeys are very much in vogue." He sniffed. And he remarked for emphasis: "I'm told that Lidgate's, butchers to the queen of England, carry the Bronze."

My friend turned to me. "Very worldly, the butchers around here. But do you think the queen of England really eats turkey? I mean, she may as well celebrate Thanksgiving. You tell me the queen of England celebrates Thanksgiving."

The butcher was sighing. He had no other customers to wait on, but he was clearly a time-is-money guy. But my friend and I were impervious. We both were interested in trying out this aberrant bird.

"Well," I smiled, "what's good enough for the queen of England is good enough for me. Besides"—I turned to my friend who was still squinting and rubbing her chin over this provocative turkey as though she were waiting for it to pale—"we can't just let this moment of culinary euphoria pass us by."

"Okay," she finally said. "This is very avant-garde for Ed and me, and"—she looked up at the butcher sharply—"I'm not entirely convinced." She was tough, this one. "But I'll take one, too."

He started to wrap up the turkeys.

"Wait a minute," snapped my friend. "What about its taste compared to, you know, the dry, white, routine turkeys that normal people eat?"

"The same or better," said the butcher.

"And cooking time?"

"The same."

"And stuffing?"

"The same." He looked weary.

So we purchased our Bronze turkeys, feeling, as the paparazzi do, a little smug and ahead of it all. Really, we rehearsed remarking to our astonished guests, white turkeys are just a bit passé.

The Broadbreasted Bronze is in fact what most people imagine when they think of turkeys. It is one of the largest strains of domesticated turkeys. Toms grow to as large as thirty-eight

pounds, and hens tend to peak at about twenty-two. Their plu-
mage is copper-bronze, with brown and black feathers in stria-
tion. Their wattles and caruncles (those bright red flaps and
nubby protrusions along their necks) are thick and full. Broadbreasted Bronzes are stately birds, the "peacock" of the turkey
breeds, with their magnificent fan tails and metallic sheen.

I hope to keep some Bronzes on my farm. I would like to
raise turkeys in some shape and form for Thanksgiving and
Christmas presents, and I'm not so keen on the white turkey—
the vernacular of commercial operations—because they are a
little ghostly-looking to me. The ones I've seen are all-over
white, with pitch-black opalescent eyes and skinny sinewy necks
and eerie rose-colored skull caps for heads. Bronzes, on the other
hand, maintain a sovereign air in the middle of all that fluff and
strut.

I have read that turkeys can be unexpectedly good company
when raised in a conducive environment. One woman who kept
a small flock of turkeys claimed they made wonderful compan-
ions and watchbirds, gobbling furiously at the sight of strangers
(actually, only toms gobble—hens cluck). They will quite happily follow you about the yard, she wrote, and run to greet you
in the mornings.

"This I have to see," said my husband.

Then I read him an account of one turkey farmer who said
her birds liked to play with a rubber ball on the lawn.

"No. Stop," he said. "We must be thinking of two different
animals."

There seem to be several turkeys out there to choose from. I
have read about Black turkeys, Slate Blue turkeys, and Narra-
gansett turkeys with deep black and gray feathers and salmon-
colored legs. There are the Bourbon Red and the Beltsville Small
White, the Crimson Dawn and the Royal Palm. Domesticated
breeds of turkey throughout the world originate from our North
American wild turkey, a truly national bird. This is one reason
why Benjamin Franklin proposed the turkey as the official bird

of the United States—"a much more respectable bird," he wrote to his daughter, than the bald eagle.

I pulled out my Murray McMurray catalogue to see what they were offering. Murray McMurray, a hatchery in Webster City, Iowa, has been around for most of this century selling and shipping poultry stock around the nation. Conveniently, they also merchandise equipment useful in poultry operations: incubators, infrared heat brooders, quail waterers, egg washers, manuals, and so on. It's one-stop shopping for many poultry enthusiasts, no less inviting for the toll-free telephone number.

I found turkeys toward the end of the catalogue, way past the bantams, past the heavy-breed chickens, past the ducks and pheasants, even past the guinea hens—those queenly polka-dotted barnyard busybodies strangely reminiscent of something from the pterodactyl era. So it was that I learned, on my way to the turkeys, that you could acquire Buff, Purple, Coral, Lavender, White, and Pearl guineas. I had only known the Pearl guineas before—black birds with a remarkably exact print of white dots across their feathers.

Guinea hens are terrific farm animals. Although these birds are noted for their meat, I know few people who would ever eat from their flock. The hens are hilarious to watch, and awfully captivating as they spend their days together, foraging your lawns for ticks, weed seeds, and the odd delectable bug. From a distance, they look like black footballs: a covey of black footballs racing at full tilt across the driveway, black footballs sitting comfortably in the sugar gum tree, black footballs *en pointe* on the stone wall, black footballs shrieking bloody murder at anyone they don't recognize. I was intrigued to imagine guineas in different colors. It was going to be hard to wait.

For turkeys, Murray McMurray was offering Broadbreasted Bronzes, Giant Whites, wild turkeys (the Eastern strain, I note for the interested aesthete), and Bourbon Reds.

"There's no denying it," I said to my husband as I scanned the page. "There is something of the buzzard in this bird."

Maybe it's the featherless head, or the blood-red cascade of wattles that dangle about the neck like primitive remnants of an entrail perhaps more judiciously left inside the body. A Darwinian oversight, in my book. McMurray's only sells turkeys in "straight run," males and females in the proportions by which they arrive. Even in this world of mankind strong-arming nature, a straight run will add up to about a fifty-fifty mix of males and females.

Having heard so much about wild turkeys, I was tempted to get a few. In the catalogue they were described as "very hardy and of course very colorful," which was compelling; and then, not "as big as the domestic turkeys but are good flyers." Did I want good flyers? Maybe another time. The Bourbon Red turkeys though, were unexpectedly alluring. The picture next to the blurb had a male and female strolling in a green meadow. It is frequently so with agricultural trade "art," that the animals depicted exude personality. He only lacked a top hat, and She was wanting her parasol. It was Sunday in the park with Tom and the little clucker. Both were deep chestnut-colored, with bold white accents on their wings and tail feathers—none of that misogynist color allocation so rife in the aviary world, where males of brilliant hues are paired with females of motley duns and grays that only ornithologists call subtle. In the turkey world, it would appear, females have plenty of rich color and equally jazzy caruncles of which to boast.

·

"A duck pond would be nice," said my husband one afternoon.

"In the wildflower meadow? Between the pear trees?"

"It would have to be covered," he said. "I don't want any Canadian geese to see it. I would have to shoot them, and the county would put me in jail."

"It's for a good cause," I said.

Canadian geese have become the bane of New England ponds, lakes, farms, and golf courses. They have proliferated during the past several years of legislated protection and, like deer, lost their favored-creature status for many Americans. I have heard from people living along the annual flyways, very civilized people who read books and prefer Mozart, strangely vicious words issuing from their lips—words like *strangle, shoot, murder, destroy, decimate*—words more at home in an angry rap tune or the Metro section of *The New York Times* than on the flagstone patio of a spacious Colonial-style house.

Flocks of Canadian geese yearly enveloped the manure piles on a farm where I once worked. They nosed out and ate undigested pieces of corn from the manure. It was a disturbing inclination. In so doing, they cleverly foiled any interest a person might have had in catching and eating one of them. I wonder if that's a Darwinian attribute. Survival of the most iron-coated stomach.

But ducks I'm fond of, and ducks we shall have on the farm. I learned from the American Minor Breeds Conservancy that the Khaki Campbell duck and the Rouen duck were considered threatened species, so I resolved to get a few to raise. And I had seen pictures of Fawn and White Runners, which are wonderfully vertical ducks with attractive (and aptly named) coloring. Those I would enjoy having around. They supposedly don't waddle, a commentary I found completely winning, and with intimations of some higher duckish gentility. Still, I don't plan to devote myself to ducks. No, the ducks, I reckon, will be largely on their own.

"You can't throw yourself into every species of livestock that the world wants to wipe out," said a friend gingerly.

"I'm not throwing myself into anything," I said. "I'm no agrarian martyr. This farm is entirely a response to my own selfish, narrow-minded, psychopathic desires. I like ducks and I like duck ponds. But ducks should be able to take care of themselves, shouldn't they? Given some food and a shoreline duck house and a second home somewhere in the Catskills."

"With that," my friend said, "I could certainly take care of myself."

I had thought little more about the duck issue until one day I went to visit the Bridgeport Zoo. Bridgeport is a city besieged. It has the garbled honor of having filed for bankruptcy as a municipality. It has a reputation for collecting the worst of inner-city problems and in no way compensating, in spite of a lovely geographical bedrock. So I felt lucky to get to the zoo before any padlocks arrived.

The zoo sprawls across a hilltop park overlooking the beautiful Naugatuck River. The usual suspects are there: wolves, deer, peacocks, bears, cats, llamas. I walked up to a kind of farm area that had a terrific mob of goats, some poultry, sheep, and a porcupine sleeping in the crook of a very young tree. Just past the snoozing porcupine was a little cement demipond, and it was there I found the most enormous duck I have ever seen. It was huge. It was beyond all duck proportions. It was swimming around in the waterweeds, probably remarking to itself that the food and the neighborhood had recently gone to hell. From the best I could make out—because all sorts of fowl were running (flapping, swimming, and waddling really) around together in the same cordoned area, and because the zoo's random explanatory placards had me completely stumped—it was a duck from China. I came home breathless.

"Have I got a duck for you!" I said to my husband. "You wouldn't believe the duck I saw today. It was gigantic—for a duck."

I had my arms open wide in narration. My husband was unmoved.

"We only have a small grill," he said.

I said, "You're missing the point. This is a fantastic animal. This guy could eat a cat for breakfast. We should really think about raising this bird."

"Well," he said, "what kind of duck is it?"

"That's the problem. I couldn't find anyone there who could tell me. The sign seemed to indicate it was from China."

"Mmmm." He frowned. "I don't want inscrutable ducks."

Part Four

Reaper

11

A Chair in
the Barn

I followed the hostage crisis in the Middle East with determination, interest, and sadness. It seems quite true that several other cultures put less value on a human life than we do in America. Well, and if the population of the world is going to reach 300 billion early into the next century, then I bet I'll put less value on a few lives, too. I already notice a black corner in my soul where the arguments in favor of capital punishment feed and thrive. There is something so dehumanizing about having so many people on this little planet that I think I have come to look upon weeding out the bad ones as a kind of sensible garden management.

Who are "the bad ones"? Who am I to judge? Quite reasonable questions, I agree. But while at one time I might have seen them as rhetorical show-stoppers, now I am apt to reply with a few candidates for culling and the acknowledgment that I am not the judge, which is the terrific luck of a lot of felons and idiots out there.

The last British and American hostages in the Middle East were finally released in the winter of 1991–1992. It seemed that, once again, so much misunderstanding, so much of the terrorists' primitivism and so many layers of confused political sediment, were responsible for the whole ordeal. Compassion mixed with my joy when I read accounts of the last men flown out of the Middle East to recuperate in Wiesbaden, Germany—not only because they had evidently suffered a good deal, but also because reintegration would be so trying. I was moved by the interview with Terry Anderson, released after a lovingly tallied 2,455 days of captivity. I read in the *International Herald Tribune* (December 7 and 8, 1991): "He told of the relatively good times, of the rich friendships he developed with fellow captives, the courses his friend Thomas M. Sutherland taught him in genetics, statistics and animal breeding, and the elaborate plans he made to start the perfect newspaper or set up the finest farm."

The finest farm, I thought. The perfect newspaper. To survive and to communicate. It was a stirringly guileless image of a soul.

The finest farm is something most farmers strive toward, most would-be farmers plan for. To some it means the highest productivity per acre, to others the most humane husbandry practices. The criteria have always been varied and contested. I have read a lot about agriculture in scientific, trade, and personal literature, and a set of definitive rules articulating the ideal husbandry has proven elusive. Instead I hear, as within a musical passage, the guiding rhythms of common sense, the cadence of seasonal changes, the bass-like beat of the basic diurnal chores.

Good agricultural reading is not easy to come by, and I rely on the trade journals for current news. Some of the magazines I have found most helpful are *American Agriculturist, Milling & Baking Weekly, Farm Journal,* and *Drovers Journal.* The USDA has a bounty of printed materials that one can summon through the Government Printing Office or state departments of agriculture. I read the newspapers and find random snippets of information. When I have sought out books about farmers and farming outside the confines of agricultural college campuses, the pickings are thin. The farm-oriented books that exist in my local library are scattered like dandelion seeds among the gardening shelves, corporate industry shelves, state history shelves, and pets shelves. Most of the literature about farmers—apart from the this-establishment-is-murdering-us ilk, or the thrillerlike tales of multinational agribusiness stratagems—seems maudlin to me. There are several books that treat farmers like a dying race of pre–Bronze Age heroes, painting them as stoic, strong, private, often Germanic (post-Bronze, these) men; a reader can almost hear the anguished sigh of the author as each page turned brings one closer to the end of the idyll.

I have found in the general farm literature a bastion of sentimentality, and it seems curiously counterpoised with the distinctly ruthless tone that characterizes what I find in most media reportage outside of the agricultural trade journals. Literature would seem to be the repository of agrarian nostalgia, whereas today's newspapers and television coverage guarantees itself a faithful audience by depicting with no measly bias the outrages of the American food production system.

When you decide to become a farmer, no matter on what scale, you're automatically jumping into the fray. Romance battles with reality. Will you do things the nice old way? Or will you partake of the modern agricultural machine? Of course, there is plenty of gray area, and you can certainly blend the best of both codes. The middle road is typically recognized as the moderate and sensible one—although it can also mean you come under fire from the woods on both sides.

If you are romantically inclined about agriculture (I hesitate to use the word *histrionic*), I think you're through as a farmer. It's easy to find delight in sheep, to find satisfaction in well-ploughed soil, but farming is a business for most people. There is money to earn and muscles to injure. There are improvements to make. There are input and output industries that push and pull upon your decisions. There are crises. There are inequities.

I wish for Terry Anderson the finest farm. He who has suffered plenty at the hands of twentieth-century primitivism, and who bore it and survived to gain an unenviable knowledge of raw human spite and transience—may he find peace on his farm. May he find the inequities of farming wonderfully banal.

·

Wherever we site the farm, there are two questions that need addressing straightaway: Can I farm, and may I farm? Indeed, it's a little late in the game for me to ask myself "Can I farm?" I've already put aside any incertitude about my own health—my allergies to alfalfa in full bloom, a physical aversion to large spiders and snakes of any size (a reaction my doctor considers entirely sound). Persisting will be the delicate issue of the health of my farmland—the quality of the soil, the inherent character of the terrain and its tenacity under seditious weather conditions. Lousy weather I regard as seditious.

As for the land itself, the first thing to do is to have the soil analyzed. One must be wary of buying land with a poor soil profile. That rings self-evident, but plenty of people do it. This contingent may be comforted by assorted success stories of land rehabilitation after the most monstrous scenarios of hazardous waste dumping and infertility. To me, the risks seem high.

A soil profile will also help me decide where to plant what, and how to fertilize, be it with chemicals, manure, cover crops, or eggshells. In the past I have enjoyed browsing the soil-sample analysis kits that they sell in hardware stores. These will alert you to the nitrogen (N), phosphorus (P), and potassium (K) levels of your ground. I prefer those boxes jam-packed with literature and 800 telephone numbers, and I steer clear of those with step-by-step printed instructions that treat you like a dummy. It's one of those mundane reminders that illiteracy in America is blooming.

N, P, and K lay the foundation for most crop fertilizers, but scores of other micronutrients are also critical in plant nourishment and soil tilth. I first learned about micronutrients in a course at Texas A&M. It was an introduction to soil sciences taught by the "marvelous Murray Milford," who sported a Marine haircut, biked to work each day on a one-speed bicycle, and learned the name of every student (a couple of hundred) in his class by the second week. He began his opening lecture with two requests: one, that baseball caps find themselves a hook outside of the auditorium, and two, that spitting (many students chewed tobacco) be suspended until after class. You could swallow in class, but you couldn't spit.

For this course, we were asked to collect a soil sample, either at random from the area or from Daddy's ranch, and to create a hypothesis with regard to it. I scooped up some dirt from the shore of nearby Lake Somerville one afternoon, having biked out there to swim, having found no living thing either in the water, of which there was little, nor some distance up the slate-colored beach, which was broad, and having thus decided that I would also not introduce my living body to the lake. I ate my yogurt, washed out the container, and scratched a quantity of this kind of shale particulate into it—it gave a new meaning to the word *beach*.

When I got back to the university, my laboratory instructor, Duane, asked me to think up a hypothesis.

I said, I just drove down to Texas two weeks ago. You tell me what you grow here.

Duane sighed. Northerners.

I said, Okay, how about I want to start a peach orchard in the vicinity?

Duane looked into my yogurt cup.

He said, You might better drill for oil.

We analyzed our soil samples for three months, and the results were as expected. No orchard. Along the way I had a wonderful time acquainting myself with the universe of nonorganic chemicals and organic matter and their interactions with water and air—from bedrock to sand, silt, and clay. Now I think about soil micronutrients with the same enthusiasm that I usually reserve for a full spice cabinet. It's not, however, a joy easily shared.

My father applies lime to his garden in the fall, out of habit now, and broadcasts his 10-10-10 fertilizer each spring. A 10-10-10 fertilizer contains ten percent nitrogen, ten percent phosphorus, and ten percent potassium.

"Which micronutrients do you suppose you have trouble with in Northampton?" I asked my father one day, my nose in a book about loams.

"Yes," he said.

"Me too," said my husband, who overheard.

Not all farmers are so abreast.

·

The second question—May you farm?—has to do with local ordinances, federal law, and environmental protection. Are there wetlands on the property? Has there been a recent sighting in your pine tree of some inexorably rare redwinged, black-billed songbird from the former Yugoslavian republic? A market basket of commercial statutes will no doubt pertain to your modest proposal to farm, and prospective farmers can begin to plumb the depths of awaiting bureaucratic stipulations with a telephone call to their community's planning and zoning commission. I did this once as an exercise when we lived in Greenwich. I called the Town Hall's Planning and Zoning department to find out how one might go about starting a farm on one's property and I was informed with firm politeness by a secretary there that such questions were the province of the local health department, to which she abruptly transferred me.

"Hmmm," said a female voice on the end of that line. "Isn't that Planning and Zoning's department?"

"One would think," I said.

She said, "Well, all I can tell you off the bat is that your animals have to be separate from your living quarters."

No cows in the house. I could accept that.

"Let me get the code out," she said. "Animal controls . . .

owners keeping or harboring more than one animal . . . no person shall build or maintain a stable or kennel within fifty feet from any house and one hundred feet from a well or watercourse or two hundred feet from a public water supply.

"Hmmm," she read on. "You have to clean the manure."

"I have to what?" I asked.

"Clean the manure, it says, so it doesn't harbor any debris. That doesn't make a lot of sense, does it? I guess it means you have to dispose of it properly, somehow. Is it dogs you're raising? If it's dogs they have to be secured, and leashes can be no shorter than ten feet in length."

"No," I said. "No kennels."

"If it's horses and you wash a horse, you have to dispose of the water somehow outside of the building." She paused. "I think that's it, as long as you keep clean—the animals I mean."

I thanked her and asked to be transferred back to planning and zoning. No one picked up the line there. Next I called the tax assessor's office.

"There's no such thing as agricultural zoning," said one of the town assessors, slightly snappish. "There's what's called farm classification. But you can't just go out and start a farm. You have to ask for a special permit for farmland from the planning and zoning commission.

"Most property," he explained, "is taxed at the rate of seventy percent of market value. To get farm classification, you have to prove to our office that you have a working farm. You have to be able to show on your Internal Revenue Service return that you got farm income. I would have to go observe the so-called farm personally."

"So," I said, "I couldn't get a tax break on my property until the farm was earning enough money to show up as income on my IRS statement."

"Correct."

"So," I said, aware that housing tracts in the community were marketed for upward of a quarter of a million dollars per acre, "it might be a few years of initial capital expenditures and overhead and no break on the property taxes."

"Correct," he said. "But it's worth pursuing. Under the 1979 valuation, a farm acre was valued at seven hundred dollars, and that value is still on the books today. It's a considerably very good deal."

It was now 1991.

"Are we still taxed under the 1979 codes?" I asked.

"Yes indeedy."

Many states have such considerably very good deals as part of an effort to preserve farmland for the public weal. There may be property-tax reductions, conservation programs, and "development rights" purchase programs whereby the state or federal government will purchase from the farmer the right to develop all or a part of that farmland into perpetuity.

I next telephoned the Connecticut Department of Agriculture in Hartford to find out where there were county extension agents who might help me through the preliminary regulatory procedures for establishing a farm. The extension service is mostly quartered in Storrs, at the University of Connecticut campus, but there are also agents working out of scattered field stations. I wasn't sure whether Connecticut even had farm management specialists. I heard that they had a spectacular horticultural department, for example, but I was nervous about their animal-science commitment.

The woman I telephoned in Hartford was in a marketing division. She had already sent me an annual report called *Connecticut Grown,* which catalogued the agricultural production statistics for the state. It was dated 1988.

"Do you have any more recent numbers than these?" I asked.

"You have 1988?" she responded. "No. Well, we've got a few numbers now for 1989. I could Xerox the sheet and send it to you . . ."

I inquired about farm management agents.

"That's a tough one," she said. "Well, we've got specialists in Bethel, for example. If you wanna grow strawberries, say, they can help you. They can tell you how far apart you plant them, okay? If you wanna grow beef, say, well they can probably help you, too."

"Yes," I said, "it's beef I'm intending to grow."

·

I am no fatalist. I used to grapple fiercely for control over my self, my life, and lose punishingly the fights I picked. Now I think less in terms of control than of a greater range of response and flexibility. I have striven to mitigate my instinctive pattern of locking all internal doors when the sirens blare, and throwing up a few impenetrable dikes. As my father once said, one is better off pursuing autonomy than autarchy. I agree with that, and I have tried.

This maturation of philosophy will be useful when I start my farm because I foresee the daily undoing of my *systems*. These are not *systems* of the technological wunderkind type, but rather concoctions of self-discipline and order within a day that is completely stripped of external blueprints. There is no how-to manual for farming. That's precisely why someone like me becomes an advice monger for years, accumulating everybody's experiences and opinions in a kettle in order to make, ultimately, my own stone soup. Comes that morning then that I wake up beside a different window, with the sun in no way bursting forth its bright encouragement but rather glowing bemusedly, waiting to see what I make of the new piece of earth I care for. Maybe there will already be a couple of sheep in the barnyard. Maybe there will already be a rooster around, rustling in his straw and preparing for another big day of mating and squabbling.

What have I gotten myself into? I will wonder in those dawns when unremembered dreams leave me beaten in my nightgown.

What shall I do first? is the better question, whether you are feeling cheerless or merry. I have learned that it is a must simply to get moving—especially so on those mornings when depression has you pinned to the mattress. Moving helps. It is a way of pushing forward that, though it sounds purely physical, seems in fact to act as a revealing metaphor for your psyche. It is as though one's body can blaze a trail forward through the huge inertia that the mind entertains.

On mornings when I feel strong, relatively doubt-free about this decision to farm, I will still need to arrange my day. I will be governor of this farm, head honcho of the hacienda, tyrant of the keep—with the usual related responsibilities. So, as a lover of patterns, I am always looking for a workable quotidian *system* that I can fall into. Suppose:

1. Feed the chickens first.
2. Feed the sheep and goats.
3. Check the cattle on pasture.
4. Fix the laying boxes.
5. Stack the new corn sacks.
6. Let the hens out and collect the eggs.
7. Clean the shed.
8. Order spring seeds.
9. Fix the south fence of the north meadow.

That makes for a good Tuesday, say, and I am such that I would enjoy the same sort of thing for Wednesday. By Wednesday, however, the corn is stacked and the vegetable seeds are already ordered. The pattern remains intact only insofar as the animals daily require feeding. What shall I fill the gaps with? No problem: four sheep need crutching and I have to get soil samples from one field to send to the extension service for analysis.

No problem. Wednesday will be great. Until, comes Wednesday morning and I find one rooster died overnight from some mysterious cause. Or maybe I notice some rats near the hay. And something is smelling odd in the goat shed. Instantly the day takes on its own momentum, overrules my *systems,* and throws me into a whirlwind of prophylactic measures. Toss those patterns out the window for today, I think. Seek them, enjoy them, and don't forget to feed the goats even on those days when the prototype fails. Try to safeguard your routines for your animals' sake—they like habits, too. And keep your sense of humor when chaos creeps like Gollum into your day.

Such is the give and take in farming. Broad patterns of routine mixed with the unpredictable particulars of mayhem. So put, farming is just a cameo for all of life. And so on the order of life's mayhem came the news one day, via my husband, that he had seen a For Sale sign that might interest me.

We had been spending some of the summer with my husband's family in northwestern Connecticut, a region we prized not so much in the 1980s when Manhattan's surplus millionaires were spilling into the area with undammable passion, but rather in the 1990s, when the money evaporated and the love affair showed its transparence and ultimately its mortality. There is beautiful farm country in this area. There are long, straight, single-lane paved roads that lead to crossroads where tall solitary oak trees stand shading old yellow houses. There are hills that pour into valleys of corn that swell into hills of grass. There are milk cows grazing—Holsteins mostly, with their imperturbable tranquility—and the colorful shingles of Black Angus breeders hung out along the road. Greenhouses are scattered beside barns, conveying that vegetable farming is taken seriously here in the land of May frosts. A man just over in Torrington raises goats I'm interested in, and I know a dairyman in Hillsdale who always shares some tips with me.

We had certainly looked at farms in the area before—picture-perfect, nestled just so, white clapboard farmhouses surrounded by meadow and two pristine barns painted red. In the last decade, those especially quaint ones were often sold to antique dealers who, with no use for the extra acreage, sold it for development—that irreversible, uncomely token of what Congress calls a healthy economy.

I found these farms as a rule spruced up and attractive, especially when I stayed in the car, way up roadside at the turnoff to the driveway. But you could tell that the woods had been creeping in without resistance for a few years, or that the little circumscribed fields of wildflowers were actually cradles of cattails, which meant marshland. A closer peek revealed the hole in the roof, the tilt of the barns, the compaction of the soil. If they were expensive to buy, they still required riches to recondition.

"I think you'll like this," said my husband, driving us over to the For Sale sign.

He handed me a newspaper clipping.

"I think you'll like this," he hummed.

Farm. Must sell. 36 Acres plus Buildings. Current lease to corn/hay production. New barn with double open stalls. No silo. Small pond. Livestock and equipment negotiable. Five minutes to railroad.

"Very tantalizing," I said. "I love distressed properties."

At the crossroads take a right, go all the way along the ridge, out of the forest, a pond is on your left, you can see Massachusetts on a clear day. We slowed. A trim little wooden sign had been staked and driven into the grass just off the road. FARM FOR SALE 36 ACRES. There was a cattle guard across the entrance. We stopped the car and stepped out to look around.

It was dead quiet up on the ridge, a Berkshire foothill. A thin pine forest to the left shimmied discreetly down the other side of the slope. Intermittent summer breezes whispered through the pines and across our ears. A katydid. A loose pebble was lifted onto the asphalt and tapped out two metallic measures of syncopation before stopping. On the right was a wooden fence that seemed to run the perimeter of the farm. It was mostly gray with age, but new brown posts here and there indicated that it was being maintained.

"I like a place that's been cared for," said my husband.

We got back into the car. There was plenty of Connecticut to see from this hilltop but the farm itself was largely invisible, tucked just over the crest.

"I love a house you can't see from the road," he said.

We drove across the cattle guard and over the rise. A serene valley stretched out below. The road curved right and downward toward a cluster of birch and copper beech trees. There the pavement petered out into a dirt farmyard, an ample circular green in the center completely shaded from the sun. The driveable path formed a circuit from farmhouse to barn to paddock and back out.

"I love shade trees," I heard beside me.

We pulled up at the house. It was a modestly proportioned, two-storey brick structure, with white shutters and nongrandiose flourishes like stone slab lintels and stone slabs under each window. There was a small porch, and the eaves of the roof seemed generously broad. I really love fat eaves. They let you keep the windows open when it rains. We wandered to the side, where we could see that the original house had been gradually added on to, chunk by pleasant chunk, guest room by kitchen by pantry, nothing too recent and mostly in white clapboards but all in concert with the initial home.

"Houses were made so sensibly then," murmured my husband.

"Hello?" I called out. I knocked on the front door but there was no answer, so we decided to make a small tour of the farmyard. The barn, painted a deep forest green, was about the same size as the house. It had a simple, lofting shape. The fronting doors to the barnyard were enormous and bolted, but a side door meant only for man and animal was open. We peered into the dark, cavernous interior. There were two double rows

of stalls on each side with a walkway down the middle, and
storage overhead on two lateral floors that made ceilings for the
stalls but kept the center alley open to the rafters. The proportions were so modest that I had to wonder who built it all. It
had a kind of European petiteness. The doorways were a perfect
height for me but would have required everyone else to stoop
—save the four-legged. I didn't mind that particularly. Like the
brick house, from the perspective of five feet and two and three-
quarters inches, it felt pleasantly sized.

A stairway down and up was at the opposite end of the barn.
We could hear gentle stamping below.

"Didn't you want a barn built into a slope?" asked my
husband.

"Have you already bought this place?" I asked in return.

We walked around the barn and then over to the paddock.
It too was in good shape, but empty. I looked out beyond the
split rail fences, beyond the inner keep of barn and house, to
hayfields, some sort of vegetable rows in a flatter tract, and the
remnants of stringing stone walls that relaxed and toppled
against the curvatures of the slopes. It was clearly a beloved
farm. I wondered who the farmer was.

My husband went to retrieve his camera from the car as I
walked down into the lower storey of the barn. From the rear,
hillside, it was open to the air but pitch-black inside from shadows and emanating a damp, cellarish cool. I crossed the cate-
gorical line from sunshine to shadow, from blanched, dry
manure and silts to black invisible earth. Such crossings are
uniquely unsettling. It's like undergoing a sentient blackout—
no swooning. It tests the memory and the mettle. Where are
you standing? On what?

As my eyes got accustomed to the dark, I stood hoping there
were no playful bulls inside unchained by ordinance of the de-
voted owner. There were certainly noises, the quick *hrumph
hrumph* breathing of a cow or pig. No, it didn't smell like pigs.
My eyes were focusing gradually and I began to see her, them.

A chestnut-brown Jersey cow was sitting out the summer heat in a bed of straw. Two trimmed Rambouillet ewes were lying next to her chewing quietly, and another younger Jersey heifer was tethered to the side wall.

"Howdy," I said aloud.

Grunts.

A few metal milk cans were glinting from back in the shadows. It was a surprisingly large space and not cut up by walls but neatly segmented by the load-bearing timbers.

"So where's the guy that runs this place?" I said. As my eyes were adjusting, I stepped deeper into the black, chatting, commenting, and enjoying the smells. This brood looked at me with glances that said they'd heard it all before, and couldn't one have peace and quiet on a hot summer day? Rusty hand tools hung on the inner walls and a few rakes and pitchforks leaned like old stray shards around the dark crevices of the barn. There were no spider webs encasing them, though. Things were used. Basic tools forever avail themselves.

"Tell me you guys take care of yourselves," I said.

A big black rubber water bucket was sitting on the stairs that led up into the main division of the barn. I turned it over and set it in the straw by the sheep. It made a dependable, not uncomfortable chair.

"Where are your buddies? There's a lot more corn stacked upstairs than you four could eat alone—not to underestimate you, of course."

A sheep nose wandered over to my knee and investigated. Never was a knee so casually rejected.

"You'd have me believe this farm was abandoned two months ago and you've been taking care of it yourselves."

Suddenly a lamb appeared from behind me and sauntered around one ewe to the other. It bent down and butted her udder, and the ewe without budging suffered it to feed. Proper sheep behavior. I looked over my shoulder to see if there were others following behind. Indeed I could now make out a small enclosure in the rear, and I thought I spotted several young lambs curled up in the straw.

"You're really bringing out your big guns now," I said.

Loud sucking noises.

"Okay, okay, I give in," I said. "Tell me what price you're offering for this place. I can't bargain anymore."

Chew, chew, chew.

"Okay, throw yourselves in and take the price down a few pegs," I said. "Just kidding. Throw yourselves in and raise the price, let's say . . . not that I wouldn't guess you're all pedigreed, but factoring in that I don't care so much, maaayyybeee. . . . Okay, maybe it's better not to talk money among friends. Why don't you just adopt me. I try never to tell the same story twice."

We sat and breathed together for a while. Then I heard my husband's voice somewhere outside. He was calling my name. I looked at the others. Men, we thought.

"Well, I should probably be going," I said.

And then I heard his voice suddenly much closer. "I saw her disappear somewhere down here."

Two tall forms appeared as silhouettes in the open entrance.

"Nora?" my husband queried the shadows.

"Yes," I said.

"Come meet Mr. Randall, the owner of the farm. There she is, Mr. Randall. I think I can just make her out. What are you doing in there, Nora?"

What could I say?

"I found a chair in the barn."

Epilogue

Very little stood between me and this farm, if you discount all the local bankers, mortgage agreements, title searches, and tithes paid to every bureaucrat and functionary who lands during this process at the desk in front of you. We spent the next few weeks considering other farms with mild interest, just to be sure, but each proved too worn, or too sterile, or too big or too remote.

I could see in this Connecticut farm a reflection of my own desire for who I might be. It was removed, but not lonely. It lacked those perfect paddocks and flawless furrows, but it expressed some lovely, empathetic gradient of wilderness restrained. The barn had a simple aesthetic I had always adored. The forest green paint on its timbers was weathering into something effortlessly beautiful and unprimped. The old house already seemed to promise a wonderful sanctuary. I envisioned it warm with music, and having a library that would rinse the day's fatigue from a reader's shoulders. The welcoming barnyard—half garden, half utility area—would allow me to be both farmer and poet. We could keep a bench there, maybe a swing, maybe take a drink out under the trees and talk about silage, apple varieties, housing for the homeless, Dickens, deworming techniques, and George Bush's acute brand of cynicism.

This farm had a kind of vanity that I liked. I say that with some reticence, because vanity is one of those major biblical sins and turns up also throughout the history of painting in horrendous allegorical apparitions. But there is to me a benign side of vanity that is not vain, that has to do with tucking in your shirt and presenting yourself with dignity.

I have learned to befriend vanity cautiously over my short lifetime. I began to see a different side of it as I watched my mother in and out of remission from Hodgkin's disease for so many years. When she was ill, her self-image slipped away into the immaterial and her vanity disappeared. She was wan, sapped, queasy. She lost her hair from the treatments. She lost her color.

Those were the years of sickness. In the intervening years of health, she would rediscover an interest in a pretty blouse, a Liberty print. She would wear her jewelry, find a new shade of lipstick. My mother was not a showy dresser, but she always aspired to a level of elegance. It was good form to dress well, she felt, however modestly, to present oneself properly. It was part of having manners, of behaving oneself in public.

"You're the only person I know," I would say, flopped on her bed in the mornings as she pulled a handkerchief from her bureau or a belt from the closet, "who overflows with understatement."

In those years when the cancer seemed defeated and her interest in the day was revived, I saw a wonderfully sound side of vanity: the smile tested in the mirror, a new pair of stockings. I carry with me, without my mother now, a sense of vanity's rubicund angles. And I felt invigorated on this Connecticut farm, which had a character that responded to my own bashful vanities.

"It will look even better when I plant banks of yellow tulips out front," I assured my husband. But he needed no reassuring.

•

So my husband and I moved through the most preliminary of official processes, and I explored an exhilarating sensation of hope and fulfillment combined. My husband's work was going well and we were altogether feeling as if we inhabited a providential oasis within the prevailing national climate of economic decline. The world outside seemed rife with mayhem, with unnegotiable obstacles and unremarked tragedies. I was surprised, then, one evening when mayhem innocently walked through our own front door.

"Something big happened today," my husband said, setting down his briefcase and settling himself on the couch.

"Good, I hope," I smiled, trying to coax his ambivalent face into something more encouraging.

"Well," he said, "they've offered me a job in Zürich. Switzerland."

I was quiet.

He said, "It sounds like a very good job."

I was having trouble speaking. If I opened my mouth, I thought, something like a primal scream would leap out before I could say anything. I pulled a jacket from our coat rack and held it to me as I remained standing in the corner by the door.

"I think we should talk about this," my husband said softly.

"Maybe I should just take a walk first," I replied. "You know." He knew. I needed a moment to collect myself. I was trying to be sensible, to prevent the outburst that was awaiting its genetic expression in every blood cell. If we talked now, I wanted to say, I'd just end up apologizing for it all later.

"But before I go," I said, "and I won't be long, I want you to know that I'm really really proud of you and of course I know you earned it." In the shadows of the corner I smiled as tenderly as I could while the tears started rolling down my cheeks.

When opportunities fling themselves in my direction, I usually acquiesce. They are not without roots, after all, in my own doing—opportunity sprouts along the path one tramples into pathdom. As for Switzerland, I was fully aware of my own contributions to this sequence of events. Living abroad had always been a dream of my husband's and mine. We had often spoken of such a chance as exciting and enriching. In a way, I suppose, there was never any question but that I would agree to go.

I cried a lot on my own time. I saw my farm suddenly slip off to a distant hill and all that went with it—the pleasures, the peace, the labor, and the struggles.

"The farm will be there when we get back," said my husband. "We will do it. I really want to see you do it." He did.

A part of me wanted to burn all the notebooks, forget the whole farm idea, and make of Switzerland a new direction to follow. I felt somehow that I had been thwarted, repulsed from agrarian life like an invader at the foot of the wall. Boiling oil and arrows from the turrets. Go home.

And home for me was perhaps the fundamental puzzle. Where was it? It was as much in the cosmopolitan cafés of Zürich's Bahnhofstrasse as within a breezy barnyard in the Berkshires. I had still spent more of my life within the comely sanctums of museums and languages than I had in the damp straw of a corral.

So many longings in life are these dull tugs from somewhere inside you. You try to identify them, you try to sate them. They are tricky to diagnose. They are like pains in the head, with their source above the left ear and their expression beneath the right eye. Depression can be such a tug, and when we get depressed we go rooting about on all different levels of our selves; we wonder whether our professional life is empty, we wonder if our spouse is unhappy, we wonder why our parents felt so emphatic about such and such. And when we find something that even remotely fits the bill—Ah yes, *that's* what must be getting me so down!—then we lunge forward to remedy the situation with the dedication of all good soldiers, with "extreme prejudice."

My longing for a farm of my own was such a dull tug. I had researched the idea for years to assure myself that this farm was really what the tug was about—if it were not at the same time a composite of so many yearnings. Having raced down many a dead end in my life, solution-seeking, I wanted this time to be more certain. And after all the inquiry I was convinced of two things: that there were no simple solutions to the inner tugs, and that I was indeed cut out for this farm, for this working preserve of the minor breeds. Moving to Europe even confirmed that for me.

That's the point at which, I think, my story became a woman's story. Women are faced throughout their lives with changes, both deliberate and unavoidable, bodily and external, that affect their whole identity. I have learned to take pride in being flexible and adroit in adapting to the next transition, although the pattern of periodic upheaval can get fatiguing.

Waiting for my farm was not something I was going to do idly in Zürich. I picked up some other threads in my basket and wove them not incongruously into my tapestry—a tapestry which, neither young nor old, is multicolored and curiously harmonious.

"You're actually pretty lucky that this move to Switzerland came before the farm," I said to my husband one day as we were enjoying an alpine view. "Moving over here would've been a difficult transition for the sheep."

He looked at me out of the corner of his eye.

"The steep slopes?" he ventured.

"The language."

He took that in. Then he said, "You imply it wouldn't have been as tough on the goats."

I sighed. "They would have refused to come."